the great
scallop
and oyster cookbook

THE GREAT SCALLOP AND OYSTER COOKBOOK

Published by:
R&R Publications Marketing Pty. Ltd
ACN 083 612 579
PO Box 254, Carlton North, Victoria 3054 Australia
Phone (61 3) 9381 2199 Fax (61 3) 9381 2689
E-mail: richardc@bigpond.net.au
Australia wide toll free: 1800 063 296

©Richard Carroll

The Great Scallop and Oyster Cookbook

Publisher: Richard Carroll
Production Manager: Anthony Carroll
Designer: Vincent Wee
Creative Director: Paul Sims
Computer Graphics: Lucy Adams
Food Photography: Gary Smith
Food Stylist: Janet Lodge
Food for Photography: Louise Hockham, Katrina Cleary
Recipe Development: Ellen Argyriou, Janet Lodge, Lyn Carroll
Proof Reader: Fiona Brodribb

The National Library of Australia
Cataloguing-in-Publication Data
The Scallop and Oyster Cookbook
Includes Index
ISBN 1 740221 54 0
EAN 9 781740 221 542

First Edition Printed July 2002
Computer Typeset in Verdana, Trojan and Charcoal

Printed in Singapore

The publishers would like to thank Mr. John Mercer of the Marine & Freshwater Resources Institute, Queenscliffe, Victoria for the provision of photographs and information relating to Scallop aquaculture used in this book.

contents

INTRODUCTION

Scallops

Scallops are one of the most delectable foodstuffs to come from the sea. Scallops are so rich, sweet and tender that a little goes a long way. Beware, however, that some unscrupulous markets may try to palm off imposter seafood as scallops. Learn how to spot a true scallop, discover its history, and try some new recipes using this seafood treat.

A Little History

The word scallop comes from the Old French *escalope* meaning 'shell', referring to the shell that houses the scallop. Scallops are mentioned in print as far back as 1280, when Marco Polo scallops as one of the seafoods sold in the marketplace in Hangchow, China. Paris restauranteur Gustave Chatagnier featured a special scallop dish on his menu in 1936.

Probably the most famous scallop dish is Coquille St. Jacques. The word *coquille* means 'shell' in French. The name of this dish has a religious history, but only in relation to the shell itself. The scallop shell was used as a badge of reverence and identification by pilgrims visiting the Spanish shrine of St James (St Jacques in French). The famous dish is made of a blend of scallops in a cream and butter sauce and is traditionally served in the beautiful shell of the scallop.

Types of Scallops

The scallop is a bivalve mollusc of the family Pectinidae. There are many varieties of scallop, ranging from the tiny, tender bay scallop to the larger, less tender deep sea scallop. The entire scallop within the shell is edible, but it is the white adductor muscle which hinges the two shells that is most commonly sold.

Oysters

Oysters are a very healthy food. They are easily digested, rich in vitamins and minerals. Oysters are highly adaptable and are currently being grown successfully in many locations.

Oysters are classified as shellfish, covered with a shell, or invertebrates, having no backbone. They are further classified as molluscs, molluscs are of soft structure and are either partially or wholly enclosed in a hard shell that is largely of mineral composition.

Research shows that oysters are low in cholesterol and high in omega-3 oils, calcium, iron, zinc and copper All shellfish have some carbohydrate in the form of glycogen. Oysters contain 3–5 percent. Oysters also contain a somewhat higher percentage of calcium than other fish and meats, which are notably low in calcium. Oysters, clams, and lobster contain more iodine than any other seafood. Few foods can compare to oysters in terms of their nutritional value.

Oysters may be purchased live in the shell, fresh or frozen shucked (removed from the shell), or canned. When alive, they have a tightly closed shell.

SCALLOP PREPARATION

A diverse and astonishing variety of univalves (abalone), bivalves (oysters, clams, mussels), crustaceans (crabs, prawns and lobsters) and cephalopods (squid and octopus) is available for our cooking pot. There is one point of concern, however, and that is the fact that once out of water, shellfish deteriorate quickly.

Step 1: After you catch some scallops, place them on ice. The cold causes the scallops to open up. In contrast, warm scallops will demonstrate quite clearly the meaning of the English verb 'to clam up'!

Step 2: With the dark side of the scallop up and the hinge facing away from you, insert a knife blade or sharpened spoon between the top and bottom shells, inserting, from the right. Cut away the muscle at its attachment to the top shell. Remove the top shell and discard.

Step 3: Remove the dark innards by gently scraping from hinge to front with a spoon or scallop knife. The innards will peel cleanly from the muscle if you carefully scrape over the muscle from hinge to front, pinching the innards against the knife or spoon with your thumb as you pass over the cut surface of the muscle.

Step 4: Now simply scrape the scallop from the bottom shell. Some people prefer to leave the muscle attached

Step 5: The limit for cleaned scallops is 1 pint per person with a maximum of ½ gallon per boat

OYSTER PREPARATION

If you use technique rather than strength, oysters are easy to open. It is best to hold the unopened oyster in a garden glove or tea towel. This will protect your hand from the rough shell) whilst you open the shell with an oyster knife, held in the other hand.

Step 1: Hold the oyster with the deep cut down and insert the tip of the oyster knife into the hinge. Twist to open the shell. Do not open oyster by attempting to insert the oyster knife into the front lip of the shell.

Step 2: Slide the oyster knife inside the upper shell to cut the muscle that attaches it to the shell. To serve, discard the upper part of shell, cut the muscle under the bottom half, then replace oyster into half shell.

Step 1

Step 2

SCALLOP FARMING

Scallop farmers require a reliable source of scallop spat (juvenile scallops) for grow-out. Spat may be collected from the wild after obtaining the necessary license, or they may be obtained from a hatchery.

Small holes are drilled in the 'ears' of the scallop shells and then suspended on a long line

Scallop Spat from the Wild

The scallop grower has a wide variety of options for culturing this species. First is the question of spat supply. The natural settling behaviour of larval scallops (spat) can be exploited by putting out collectors which simulate the conditions in which scallops would normally choose to set. Collectors are made by stuffing bundles of nylon fishing net into onion bags with a mesh size of 2–3mm.

These bags are anchored in the ocean a few meters above the bottom in a location where scallop larvae may be expected to settle. They are set out in the fall shortly before the larvae reach the pediveliger stage. This can be determined by taking plankton samples and checking the development of the larvae. The collectors are usually left in the water until the following summer. The larvae will have grown to 8–10 mm diameter, and will be large enough to handle.

Hatchery Culture

The alternative to collecting wild spat is to raise the larvae in a hatchery. Adult scallops are brought into the hatchery and conditioned by feeding them a mixture of several species of phytoplankton. Part of the success of a hatchery lies in growing sufficient phytoplankton and in feeding it to the scallops at an optimum quality. Water quality control is also important at all stages of the hatchery operation.

Eggs released by the females are captured on fine mesh screens and transferred to large tanks where the water is changed regularly and the tanks kept scrupulously clean. After hatching, the larvae are fed mixtures of cultured algae. Settling is done on rigid plastic sheeting or fiberglass panels suspended in the tanks.

Culture of Post-Settled Scallops

Post-settled larvae may be held on screen-bottom trays. Warm water containing cultured algae is pumped to them. The most successful technique is one called an upweller. Screen-bottom trays or cylinders containing the spat are suspended in a tank into which water is pumped.

Intermediate Grow-out

When juvenile scallops are 5–10mm in diameter they are ready for transfer to intermediate grow-out.

At this stage they are about one year old. Intermediate grow-out is usually done in fine mesh lantern nets or pearl nets. These are suspended on long lines deep enough in the water to be below the action of surface waves.

Long lines consist of a length of polythene rope anchored firmly at each end. The lines have floats and ballast weights to keep the line suspended just far enough below the surface to avoid the wave action. Scallops do not like to be jiggled. The farmer's secret is to find a site where there is good water exchange and a good supply of plankton and where temperatures are suitable.

Final Grow-out

Farmers have several options for grow-out. The so-called Chinese lantern net or variants of it developed by individual growers is commonly used. Scallops are loaded into the different levels and the nets are suspended in mid-water as before. As the scallops grow they are thinned into larger mesh nets. The secret is to have a mesh just small enough to prevent the escape of the scallops, and large enough to maximize water exchange.

An alternative is to pass loops or plastic toggles through small holes drilled in the 'ears' of the scallop shell and suspend them from the long line. This can be done when the scallops are as small as 30mm in diameter, but the operation is delicate.

Tending the long lines is done either from a boat which hauls the line to the surface, or by divers who clip on, or remove nets from the long-line underwater.

A fourth option is for the scallops to be scattered on the bottom for harvest by conventional fishing techniques, or by divers. In this

One year old scallops suspended in a mesh lantern

case growth to market size may take longer and mortality is higher, particularly among small scallops.

Growth varies from site to site, and there is also much variation in growth rate between individual scallops. Nevertheless, scallops in suspended culture have been grown to marketable size in 18 months to 2 years. Growth is more rapid than when scallops are on the bottom, and loss to predators is much reduced.

OYSTER FARMING

Stick and Tray Culture

Stick and tray culture is the most common method of oyster farming. Stock depends on natural spatfall, which is collected on tarred and concreted hardwood sticks. These are 1.8m long and 2.5cm/1in square.

The sticks are placed in their catching areas between the end of December and mid-February. The sticks are attached to two horizontal, parallel runners, 2.5cm/1in wide, 5cm/2in tall and 1.2m long. Twelve sticks are attached to the runners, then they are placed in pairs with the sticks both facing inwards, leaving a 2.5cm/1in gap between each stick. The gap is wide enough to allow the spat to grow strong, but thin enough to stop predators.

At this time the sticks are separated into stacks with non-paired racks. This thins the oysters out, allowing more food per oyster. They are left like this for 7–8 months, when they are further separated into single sticks and left a further for about 6–12 months, after time which they are harvested by hitting the stick with a hammer to shake off the oysters.

The oysters are then put loose in trays for about 9 months or more to fatten. From here they are purified, sorted and then sold. By the time they are sold the oysters will be 3–4 years old.

Single-Seed Culture

This involves using spat collected specially for the purpose of single-seed culture. These are collected using normal sticks or PVC plastic collectors.

The spat are put in trays or cylinders. The trays allow growing space for the oyster to grow to a cup shape. In cylinders, the action of the tide rolls the cylinder around a pole, affecting the growth to produce a cupped oyster. If the oysters are grown for too long with this method then they will become soft shelled, and undesirable.

Sub-Tidal Culture

Oysters grown with this type of culture generally grow faster than inter-tidally grown oysters because they spend all of their time underwater, meaning they can feed more often. Their condition also recovers more quickly after spawning than inter-tidally grown oysters.

Rafts

This is the preferred method for cultivating oysters in Japan. The stacks are usually stocked with oysters that will be marketable before fouling becomes excessive.

Pontoons

This method uses PVC pipes (6m long by 10cm wide) glued together and capped to form floats 18–24m long. The pipes are used in pairs to support sticks or trays. The sticks can be submerged for 8–12 months, after which they are knocked off and grown in trays. The stick cannot be lifted out of the water to kill off fouling because the handling would bump off too many oysters.

Dredge Bed culture

This is used in the USA. The operation is simple: a layer of oyster shells is deposited on hard, clean bottoms of estuaries; the spat then collects and grows on this; and the oysters are harvested by systematically dredging the bottom with a small dredger (about 1m wide).

APPETISERS & SNACKS

Lemon and Herb Basted Scallops

INGREDIENTS

4 tablespoons butter, melted

2 tablespoons lemon juice

1 clove garlic, crushed

1 teaspoon basil, finely chopped

1 teaspoon coriander, finely chopped

1 teaspoon mint finely chopped

500g/18oz package frozen scallops

1 red onion, cut into wedges

1 red capsicum, cut into triangles

watercress

lemon wedges

METHOD

1. Combine the butter, lemon juice, garlic and herbs and set aside.

2. Thread scallops, onion and capsicum onto skewers and brush with the butter mixture.

3. Place the skewers onto a preheated grill plate turning once and brushing with butter mixture, until scallops are just cooked (approximately 5 minutes).

3. Serve garnished with watercress and lemon wedges.

Serves 6

Devilled Oysters

INGREDIENTS

12 small oysters, shucked

1 tablespoon red wine vinegar

1 teaspoon Worcestershire sauce

a few drops Tabasco sauce

30g/1oz butter

1 shallot, finely chopped

1 clove garlic, crushed

55g/2oz piece pancetta
   or smoked bacon, finely chopped

55g/2oz fresh white breadcrumbs

2 tablespoons freshly grated
   Parmesan cheese

1 tablespoon fresh parsley, chopped

a little olive oil

salt and pepper

METHOD

1. Carefully strain the juices from the oysters into a bowl and stir in the vinegar, Worcestershire sauce and Tabasco sauce. Cut through the muscle that attaches the oyster to the deep half of the shell, but leave the oysters in the shell. Discard the other half of the shell.

2. Melt the butter in a small pan and fry the shallot and garlic for 5 minutes. Add the pancetta or bacon and stir-fry for a further 3–4 minutes until browned.

3. Add the breadcrumbs and pour in the oyster juice mixture. Boil until the liquid has nearly all evaporated. Remove from the heat and stir in the Parmesan and parsley and season to taste with salt and pepper. Leave to cool.

4. Arrange the oysters in a baking dish and top each one with the breadcrumb mixture. Drizzle over a little olive oil and cook under a preheated grill for 3–4 minutes until bubbling and golden. Serve at once.

Serves 6

LEMON AND HERB BASTED SCALLOPS

Scallop and Green Bean Terrine

INGREDIENTS

285g/10oz sea scallops, rinsed
1 tablesppon egg white, lightly beaten
1 teaspoon salt
1/4 teaspoon white pepper or to taste
1/8 teaspoon nutmeg
225g/8oz green beans, trimmed
  and cut into 1/4in/5mm inch pieces
2 tablespoons unsalted butter, softened
11/4 cups Créme fraiche
1/3 cup Parmesan cheese, grated
3/4 cup tomato coulis (see below)

Tomato Coulis
400g/14oz can crushed tomatoes
1 onion, chopped
1 teaspoon butter
1 tablespoon crushed garlic
1/8 teaspoon dried sage

METHOD

1. In a food processor with a metal blade, puree the scallops with the egg white, salt, white pepper, and nutmeg. Transfer the puree to a metal bowl and chill, covered, for 1 hour. In a saucepan, blanch the green beans in boiling salted water, for 6 minutes. Drain.

2. Toss the beans with 1 tablespoon butter, season them with salt and white pepper to taste and set aside. Set the bowl of puree in a larger bowl of ice water. Beat in 1 cup of creme fraiche, 1/4 cup at a time, until it is incorporated and the mousse is fluffy.

3. Fold in the green beans and spoon the mousse into a buttered terrine. Place terrine in a baking pan and add enough hot water to reach 2/3 the way up the side of the terrine.

4. Bake, covered with a buttered sheet of wax paper and the lid or a double layer of foil, in a preheated 190°C/375°F oven for 45 minutes. Remove terrine from pan, remove lid and paper, and allow to cool for at least 30 minutes. Cut into 6 slices and arrange slices in a buttered gratin dish just large enough to hold them in one layer. Spread some of the remaining butter lightly over each slice and sprinkle with Parmesan cheese.

5. Bake in a preheated 200°C/400°F oven for 20–25 minutes, or until they are hot and puffed slightly. In a saucepan, combine the tomato coulis and the remaining créme fraiche. Heat the sauce over moderate heat, stirring, until it is heated through. Serve in a boat alongside the terrine.

Tomato Coulis
Sauté the onion and garlic over low heat until translucent. Add tomatoes and seasonings and simmer until most of the moisture has evaporated (should be the consistency of thick sauce).

Serves 6

Scallop Puffs

INGREDIENTS

250g/9oz sea scallops

¼ cup/55mL/2fl oz mayonnaise

¼ cup freshly grated Gruyère cheese

½ teaspoon Dijon-style mustard

1 teaspoon fresh lemon juice

1 tablespoon finely
  chopped fresh parsley leaves

1 large egg white

1 sheet puff pastry
  cut into 25 squares, 5cm X 5cm/
  2in X 2in

salt and pepper

METHOD

1. Place the scallops in a saucepan with enough salted water to cover them completely. Bring the water to a simmer, and poach the scallops for 5 minutes. Drain the scallops well and cut them into 1cm/½in pieces.

2. In a bowl, whisk together the mayonnaise, Gruyére, mustard, lemon juice, parsley, and salt and pepper to taste. Add the scallops, and toss the mixture well. In a small bowl beat the egg white until it just holds stiff peaks and fold it into the scallop mixture, gently but thoroughly.

3. Place pastry squares, that have been pricked with a fork, onto a lined oven tray and bake at 100°C/200°F for 5 minutes, or until just turning golden.

4. Remove from oven, and place a heaped teaspoon of the scallop mixture onto each pastry square.

5. Place under a preheated grill, until the topping is bubbling and lightly golden, taking care not to burn the edges of the pastry.

Makes 32 hors d'oeuvres

Oysters in Tempura Batter

INGREDIENTS

20 oysters
sunflower oil for deep frying

Dipping Sauce
4 tablespoons dark soy sauce
4 tablespoons water
juice of 1 lime

Tempura Batter
55g/2oz cornflour
55g/2oz plain flour
small pinch salt
4 teaspoons toasted sesame seeds
170mL/6fl oz ice cold soda water
lime wedges to serve

METHOD

1. Open all the oysters and pour off the liquid. Carefully cut the meat out of the deeper shells and retain the shells for serving.

2. Mix together the ingredients for the dipping sauce and pour into 4 dipping saucers.

3. Heat some oil for deep frying to 190°C/370°F.

4. Make the batter by sifting the cornflour, flour and salt into a mixing bowl. Stir in the sesame seeds then stir in the ice cold soda water until combined just mixed. Add a little more water if it seems too thick. The batter should be very thin and almost transparent.

5. Dip the oysters, one at a time. Drop into the hot oil and fry for minute until crisp and golden. Lift out and drain on absorbent paper.

6. Return the oysters to their shells and arrange on plates. Serve with lime wedges and dipping sauce.

Serves 4

Oyster Kebabs

INGREDIENTS

1 large bottle fresh oysters
plain flour, salt and pepper
12 bamboo skewers (soaked in
   water for 30 minutes)
2 eggs, lightly beaten
2 cups fresh breadcrumbs
2 tablespoons parsley flakes
oil for deep frying

Seafood Sauce
4 tablespoons thickened cream
1 tablespoon tomato sauce
1 tablespoon lemon juice
2 tablespoons Worcestershire sauce
dash tabasco sauce
1/2 teaspoon horseradish cream
pinch dry mustard
salt and cracked black peppercorns

METHOD

1. Drain oysters and toss in seasoned flour. Gently push oysters onto bamboo skewers.

2. Coat kebabs in beaten egg, then roll in breadcrumbs combined with parsley flakes.

3. Heat oil in frying pan. Fry quickly for about 1 minute (or until crumbs are golden).

4. Serve with seafood sauce.

5. To make seafood sauce, combine all ingredients thoroughly.

Serves 4–6

Oyster Spring Rolls

INGREDIENTS

oil

2 tablespoons grated fresh ginger
   or shredded pickled ginger

1 tablespoon chopped
   fresh coriander or dill

1 tablespoon finely
   chopped chives or green onions

1 teaspoon lime or lemon juice

5 sheets spring roll pastry
   wrappers or 20 wonton wraps

20 fresh oysters, shucked
   or 1 jar (about 20 oysters) drained

Dipping Sauce

1 green onion, sliced diagonally

2 tablespoons rice wine vinegar

2 tablespoons reduced-salt soy sauce

1 tablespoon lime or lemon juice

METHOD

1. Preheat oven to 180°C/350°F. Lightly spray or brush a baking tray with unsaturated oil.

2. To make dipping sauce, place green onion, vinegar, soy sauce and lime juice in a small serving bowl. Mix to combine and set aside.

3. Place ginger, coriander, chives and lime juice in a small bowl. Mix to combine.

4. Cut each sheet of spring roll pastry into four squares. Place an oyster on the centre of each square. Top with a little of the ginger mixture. Brush edges with water. Fold in sides and roll up.

5. Place rolls, seam side down, on prepared baking tray. Bake for 10–12 minutes or until pastry is crisp and golden. Serve with dipping sauce.

Makes 20 mini spring rolls

Scallop and Prawns en Brochette

INGREDIENTS

225g/8oz pickling onions

6 bacon rashers

455g/1lb green prawns,
  peeled, deveived, tail intact

400g/14oz scallops

2 tablespoons olive oil

55g/2oz melted butter

2 tablespoons fresh dill, chopped

2 tablespoons parsely, chopped

2 spring onions, finely chopped

2 cloves garlic, crushed

freshly ground black pepper

2 teaspoons grated lemon rind

2 tablespoons lemon juice

METHOD

1. Parboil onions until almost tender. Drain and rinse under cold water. Remove rind from bacon, cut each rasher into 3 and roll each section up.

2. Thread prawns, scallops and bacon onto skewers. Finish with an onion on the end of each one.

3. Combine oil, butter, dill, parsley, spring onions, garlic, pepper, lemon rind and juice. Pour over seafood skewers and marinate for at least 1 hour.

4. Remove from marinade cook on preheated barbecue grill until tender, brushing occasionally with marinade.

Serves 6

Scallops Baked in Filo with Lemon Butter

INGREDIENTS

Sauce

1 tablespoon butter

2 tablespoons minced shallot

1/2 cup/125mL/4fl oz dry white wine

2 tablespoons whipping cream

Scallops

6 filo pastry sheets

1/2 cup/125mL/4fl oz melted butter

8 large sea scallops

1 tablespoon brandy

METHOD

Sauce

1. Melt butter in small heavy saucepan over medium heat.

2. Add shallot and sauté 3 minutes.

3. Add wine and boil for 5 minutes or until liquid is reduced to 1/4 cup.

4. Stir in cream.

Scallops

1. Place 1 filo sheet on work surface (keep remaining filo covered). Brush with butter.

2. Top with second sheet. Brush with butter.

3. Top with third sheet. Cut filo stack into four 15cm/6in squares.

4. Place one scallop in center of each square. Brush scallops with brandy. Season with salt and pepper.

5. Pull up all sides of filo around scallops to form pouches. Pinch center to seal.

6. Arrange pouches on baking sheet. Brush with melted butter.

7. Preheat oven to 220°C/425°F. Bake pouches for 10 minutes or until golden.

8. Re-heat sauce over medium-low heat. Whisk in yolk; do not boil. Add butter and whisk until just melted. Add lemon juice and season with salt and pepper. Spoon sauce onto plates and top with pastry pouches.

Serves 4

SCALLOPS BAKED IN FILO WITH LEMON BUTTER

Gratin of Scallops and Mushrooms

INGREDIENTS

4 large fresh scallops

145mL/5fl oz milk

145mL/5fl oz double cream

30g/1oz plain flour

30g/1oz butter

1/4 teaspoon freshly grated nutmeg

55g/2oz Gruyere or Lancashire cheese diced

115g/4oz button mushrooms trimmed & halved

2 tablespoons butter, extra

METHOD

1. Trim the scallops, remove the orange coral and cut the white flesh of each scallop into 8 pieces.

2. Pour the milk into a non-stick saucepan. Add the scallops (except for the corals), bring to the boil and simmer for 5 minutes. Remove the scallops from the milk and set aside.

3. Add the cream, flour, butter, and nutmeg and whisk gently over a low heat until the sauce thickens. Add the cheese and allow to melt without letting it boil.

4. Sauté mushrooms in the extra butter for 2–3 minutes.

5. Spoon some scallops onto the center of each serving plate. Arrange mushrooms around the scallops. Drizzle any juices over the mushrooms.

6. Top scallop pieces with corals and pour overheated sauce.

Serves 4

Skewered Scallops in Orange Butter

INGREDIENTS

500g/18oz fresh scallops

Orange Butter
125g/4¹/₂oz butter
1 teaspoon brown sugar
2 teaspoon orange zest
¹/₃ cup orange juice

METHOD

1. Remove any brown membrane from the scallops and rinse well. Leave the coral attached. Pat dry with paper towel and thread onto metal skewers.

2. Melt the butter in the microwave of a saucepan and stir in the remaining ingredients. Brush over the skewered scallops.

3. Cook under a hot grill for 2 minutes each side, brushing with the orange butter as they cook.

4. Place on serving plate and pour over the remaining hot melted butter. Serve immediately.

Serves 4

Note: The skewered scallops may also be cooked on the barbecue or char grill. Cook for 1 minute each side when place on direct heat.

SCALLOPS & OYSTERS IN THEIR SHELLS

Grilled Oysters with Champagne and Cream

INGREDIENTS

12 fresh oysters

3 tablespoons champagne, dry sparkling wine or dry vermouth

30g/1oz butter

2 tablespoons double cream

black pepper

115g/4oz baby spinach

METHOD

1. To open each oyster, place a thick cloth on a work surface and put the shell on top, flat side up. Wrap a cloth around your hand and insert a small sharp knife between the shell halves, opposite the hinge. Taking care not to cut yourself, work the knife back and forth to loosen the muscle attached to the inside of the flat shell, then prise open. Scoop out each oyster with a teaspoon and strain the juices into a small saucepan. Remove and discard the muscle from the 12 rounded half-shells, then wash and dry the shells. Place in a flameproof dish lined with crumpled foil so that the shells sit level.

2. Bring the oyster juices to a simmer and poach the oysters for 30–60 seconds, until just firm. Remove from the pan. Add the champagne to the pan and boil for 2 minutes to reduce. Remove from the heat and whisk in the butter, then the cream. Season with pepper.

3. Preheat the grill to high. Cook the spinach in a saucepan for 2–3 minutes, until wilted. Squeeze out the excess liquid and divide between the shells. Top with an oyster and spoon over a little sauce. Cook close to the grill for 1 minute or until heated through.

Serves 4

Poached Scallops with Ginger and Spring Onion

INGREDIENTS

500g/18oz fresh scallops

4 spring onions

1 medium carrot

4 sprigs continental parsley

3/4 cup water

1/4 cup lemon juice

1 teaspoon soy sauce

2 teaspoons honey

2 teaspoons grated fresh ginger root

METHOD

1. Remove any dark membrane from the scallops leaving coral attached. Rinse well.

2. Wash and peel spring onions and carrot, cut into julienne strips. Pluck the parsley leaves from the stalks and rinse.

3. Heat water, lemon juice, soy sauce, honey and ginger to simmering point. Add the scallops julienne strips and parsley and poach for 3–4 minutes. Do not overcook.

4. Remove to individual scallop shells or entrée dishes with a slotted spoon. Strain the poaching liquid, return to the saucepan and reduce over quick heat to intensify the flavour. Spoon over the scallops and serve immediately

Serves 4

Oysters Rockefeller

INGREDIENTS

rock salt

12 medium oysters in shell

2 tablespoons onion, finely chopped

2 tablespoons parsley, chopped

2 tablespoons celery, finely chopped

1/4 cup butter (or margarine)

1/2 cup chopped fresh spinach

1/3 cup dry bread crumbs

1/4 teaspoon salt

7 drops red pepper sauce

dash ground anise

METHOD

1. Fill two 23cm/9in glass pie dishes with rock salt to 1cm/1/2 in deep; sprinkle with water. Scrub oysters in shell under running cold water. Break off thin end of shell with hammer. Force a table knife or shucking knife between shell at broken point; pull apart. Cut oyster at muscle to separate from shell.

2. Remove any bits of shell and place oyster on deep half of shell. Arrange filled shells on rock salt bases. Heat oven to 230°C/450°F. Cook, onion, parsley and celery in butter, stirring constantly, until onion is tender.

3. Mix in remaining ingredients. Spoon about 1 tablespoon spinach mixture onto each oyster. Bake 10 minutes.

Serving of 12 oysters

Oysters Acapulco

INGREDIENTS

24 oysters (or clams or mussels)
  on the half shell
rock salt (optional)
$1/4$ cup coriander pesto
$1/2$ cup finely diced red capsicum
$1/2$ cup crumbled cacique
  or feta cheese

Coriander pesto

$1^1/2$ cups coriander leaves
$1/4$ cup pinenuts, toasted
2 cloves garlic, roughly chopped
$1/4$ cup Parmesan cheese, grated
$1/4$ cup pecorino cheese, grated
75mL/$2^1/2$fl oz olive oil
salt and freshly ground black pepper

METHOD

1. Heat grill. If grilling oysters, make a bed
of rock salt in 2 baking pans and arrange
the oysters in them.
(If barbecueing, the oysters will go directly
on the grill.) Prepare the coriander pesto.

Coriander pesto

1. Place the coriander, pinenuts, garlic and
cheeses in a food processor, and process,
until a paste.With the motor still running, add
oil in a steady stream, until well combined.

2. Season with salt and pepper, to taste.
Store in fridge, with a little olive oil over
top, to prevent coriander going brown.

Makes $3/4$ cup of pesto
Serving of 24 oysters

Oysters Greta Garbo

INGREDIENTS

3 dozen natural oysters in shells

juice of 1/2 lime or lemon

6 slices smoked salmon
   (cut into fine strips)

1 cup/250mL/9fl oz sour cream

2 tablespoons fresh chives
   chopped for garnish

red caviar for garnish

crushed ice for serving

METHOD

1. Sprinkle the oysters with lime juice and top with smoked salmon.

2. Put a dollop of the sour cream onto each oyster.

3. Garnish with chives and red caviar. Serve on a bed of ice.

Serves 6 (as an entrée)

Oysters and Mussels in Shells

INGREDIENTS

500g/18oz mussels, scrubbed and
   beards removed

24 oysters in half shells

55g/2oz butter, softened

1 tablespoon fresh parsley, chopped

2 tablespoons lemon juice

1 tablespoon orange juice

1 tablespoon white wine

METHOD

1. Preheat barbecue to a high heat. Place mussels and oysters on barbecue grill and cook for 3–5 minutes or until mussel shells open and oysters are warm. Discard any mussels that do not open after 5 minutes of cooking.

2. Place butter, parsley, lemon juice, orange juice and wine in a heavy-based saucepan. Place on barbecue and cook, stirring, for 2 minutes or until mixture is bubbling.

3. Place mussels and oysters on a serving platter, drizzle with butter mixture and serve immediately.

Serves 6

Note: Mussels will live out of water for up to 7 days if treated correctly. To keep mussels alive, place them in a bucket, cover with a wet towel and top with ice. Store in a cool place and as the ice melts, drain off the water and replace ice. It is important that the mussels do not sit in the water or they will drown.

OYSTERS GRETA GARBO

Chardonnay Oysters

INGREDIENTS

36 freshly opened oysters
crushed ice

Chardonnay Vinaigrette
3 spring onions, finely sliced
1/3 cup/85mL/3fl oz dry chardonnay wine
2 tablespoons cider vinegar
1 tablespoon light vegetable oil
crushed black peppercorns to taste

METHOD

1. Arrange oysters on a serving platter lined with crushed ice.

2. To make vinaigrette, place spring onions, wine, vinegar, oil and black peppercorns in a bowl and whisk to combine. Just prior to serving, spoon a little vinaigrette over each oyster.

Serves 6

Oysters Kilpatrick

INGREDIENTS

24 oysters on the shell
1 teaspoon Worcestershire sauce
1 cup/250mL/9fl oz cream
pepper and salt
250g/9oz bacon rashers, finely chopped
fine breadcrumbs

METHOD

1. Remove oysters from shells and put aside.
Put shells on a baking sheet and heat in a
moderate oven. Mix Worcestershire sauce and
cream. When shells are hot, return oysters to
shells. Use tongs to handle the shells, as they
get very hot. Add a little of the cream mixture
to each shell and sprinkle with pepper and salt.

2. Top each oyster with chopped bacon and
fine breadcrumbs. Place baking sheet under a
hot grill and grill until bacon is crisp but not
burnt and oysters are warmed through.

3. Oysters Kilpatrick are very tasty served
with a bowl of hot puréed spinach and thin
slices of buttered brown or rye bread.

Serves 2–4 as an entrée

Scallops with Mango Salsa

INGREDIENTS

16 scallops in half shells
freshly ground black pepper

Mango Salsa
1 mango, peeled and chopped
1 tablespoon fresh mint, chopped
1 tablespoon lemon juice
2 tablespoons sesame seeds, toasted

METHOD

1. To make salsa, place mango, mint, lemon juice and sesame seeds in a small bowl and mix to combine. Cover and refrigerate until required.

2. Bring a large saucepan of water to the boil. Add scallops and cook for 1 minute or until tender. Using a slotted spoon, remove scallops from water and place on a serving platter. Serve warm or chilled, seasoned with black pepper and topped with salsa.

Makes 16

Oysters with Gravlax

INGREDIENTS

**250g/9oz gravlax or smoked salmon
slices
16 oysters in the shell
3 tablespoons lemon juice
freshly ground black pepper**

METHOD

1. Cut gravlax or smoked salmon into long
strips. Loosen oysters in shells.

2. Top oysters with gravlax or smoked salmon
slices. Sprinkle with lemon juice and season
with black pepper. Cover and refrigerate until
required.

Scallops Baked
with Cured Ham

INGREDIENTS

2 tablespoons olive oil

500g/18oz scallops, in half shell

salt and freshly ground black pepper

$1/2$ cup minced onion

1 garlic clove, minced

**$1/4$ cup minced cured ham, such as
proscuitto**

3 tablespoons dry white wine

$1/2$ cup breadcrumbs

1 tablespoon minced parsely

1 teaspoon lemon juice

METHOD

1. Heat 1 tablespoon oil in a large skillet
and sauté the scallops over high heat for
1 minute. Divide the scallops among the
shells and sprinkle with salt and pepper.

2. Add the onion and garlic and a little more
oil, if necessary, to the skillet. Cover and
cook over low heat for 15 minutes. Add the
ham and sauté 1 minute. Stir in the wine
and let it cook off. Spoon mixture over
scallops. Pre-heat the oven to 230°C/450°F.

3. In a small bowl, combine the bread
crumbs, parsley, lemon juice and remaining
oil. Sprinkle over the scallops. Place shells
on baking sheet and bake 10 minutes. If
necessary, run under the grill to brown
the top crumbs.

Serves 2 or 4 as tapas

Hot Oysters and Leeks

INGREDIENTS

20–24 large oysters in the half shell

coarse sea salt

1 small leek, washed and finely sliced

30g/1oz butter

salt, pepper and a pinch of sugar

squeeze of lemon juice

1/2 cup/125mL/4 1/2fl oz dry white wine

pinch of saffron threads

   or curry powder

1/2 cup/125mL/4 1/2fl oz cream

1 egg yolk

METHOD

1. Remove the oysters from their shells and keep chilled. Wash the shells and arrange in 4 individual gratin dishes, on a bed of course sea salt to keep them level.

2. Wash leek and slice it finely. Melt butter in a pan and toss the leek in the hot butter. Season with salt, freshly ground pepper and sugar, cover tightly and cook gently until tender. Season with lemon juice.

3. Boil the wine with the saffron or curry powder over a moderate heat until reduced by half. In a small bowl combine the cream with the egg yolk and whisk. Whisk in the hot wine mixture and return to gentle heat to thicken slightly, whisking all the time. Do not let it boil. Add salt and white pepper to taste and remove from heat.

4. Arrange the cooked leeks in the oyster shells and place oysters on top. Coat each oyster with the sauce and place under a preheated hot grill for a minute or so to glaze. Serve immediately.

Serves 4

Steamed Scallops with Black Beans and Garlic

INGREDIENTS

12 large scallops (or 24 small scallops)

1 tablespoon dry sherry

1 tablespoon Chinese salted black beans

1 teaspoon freshly crushed garlic

3 teaspoons soy sauce

1/4 teaspoon salt

pinch cracked black peppercorns

1/2 teaspoon sugar

1 teaspoon oil

1 teaspoon cornflour

1/4 teaspoon oriental sesame oil

1 spring onion (green part only)
  cut into fine slices

12 coriander leaves

1/2 hot chilli seeded and cut into

5mm/1/4 in diamond shapes

METHOD

1. Use the 12 scallop shells for the cooking and serving dishes. Mix scallops with the sherry, and then place one scallop in each shell. Set aside.

2. Soak the black beans covered in cold water for 15 minutes, then rinse, dry on paper towels, and mince. Combine beans, garlic, soy sauce, salt, pepper, sugar, oil and cornflour. Distribute some of this mixture over each of the scallops, and trickle the sesame oil over each scallop.

3. Bring a few inches of water to a vigorous boil in a steamer. Place the scallops on a steamer rack, cover tightly, and steam for 5 minutes. Remove, sprinkle with spring onions, and garnish each scallop with one coriander leaf and a hot chilli diamond before serving.

Serves 4

Oysters Bloody Mary

INGREDIENTS

6 scrubbed oysters, opened

splash of vodka

dash of Tabasco sauce

grind of black pepper

squeeze of fresh lime

**flesh of 2 fresh tomatoes,
    chopped (no pulp or seeds)**

**$1/2$–1 teaspoon whole grain
    mustard (optional)**

METHOD

1. Combine the ingredients and spread evenly over the opened oysters. Chill or grill for 5–10 minutes. Serve with bread and butter, or hot buttered toast. Ensure extra lime and pepper are available.

Serving of 6 oysters

SEAFOOD SOUPS

Creamy Scallop Soup with Mushroom-Asparagus Duxelles

INGREDIENTS

2 tablespoons butter

2 shallots, minced

250g/9oz mushrooms (reserve one), minced

8 spears asparagus (reserve tips), minced

2 tablespoons flour

4 cups milk

concentrated fish (or scallop) stock, which would dilute to 4 cups

250g/9oz ocean scallops, cut into bite-sized pieces

reserved asparagus spears

reserved mushroom, cut into 8 thin slices

1/2 cup double cream

1/4 cup dry white wine

pinches of paprika to garnish

METHOD

1. In a saucepan, melt butter, add minced shallots, minced mushrooms, and minced asparagus, and saute on low heat for 10 minutes, stirring from occasionaly. When flavours are concentrated, stir in the flour and cook for a minute or two, then slowly whisk in the milk. When the soup begins to thicken, whisk in the fish or seafood stock and let simmer for a minute or two.

2. Add the scallops, reserved asparagus tips, and reserved mushroom slices and simmer for 3 minutes. Pour in the double cream, reheat, and simmer for a few more minutes.

3. When ready to serve, pour in the wine, then ladle the soup into soup bowls, evenly dividing the scallops, mushroom slices, and asparagus tips. Garnish with a pinch of fresh paprika and serve immediately.

Serves 4

Creamy Oyster Bisque

INGREDIENTS

20 fresh oysters, shucked or 1 jar drained,
liquid reserved
low-salt fish or vegetable stock
1/2 cup white wine
1 small white onion or 1/2 leek, diced
1 stalk celery, diced
2 cups diced peeled potato
1 tablespoon chopped fresh thyme or 1
teaspoon dried thyme
1/2 cup low-fat milk
freshly ground black pepper
sprigs watercress or fresh parsley, optional

METHOD

1. Measure liquid from oysters. Add stock to make up to 1 cup/250 mL/9fl oz.

2. Heat 2 tablespoons of the wine in a large saucepan over a low heat. Add onion and celery. Cook, stirring, for 4–5 minutes or until onion is transparent. Add potato and thyme. Stir in stock mixture and remaining wine. Bring to boil and. simmer for 10–15 minutes or until potatoes are soft and most of the liquid is absorbed. Cool slightly.

3. Transfer mixture to a food processor or blender. Add half the oysters, the milk and black pepper to taste. Purée. Return mixture to a clean saucepan. Bring to the boil. Remove soup from heat and stir in remaining oysters.

4. To serve, ladle soup into warm bowls and top with watercress or parsley sprigs, if desired.

Serves 4

CREAMY OYSTER BISQUE

Irish Oyster Soup

INGREDIENTS

2 large potatoes, unpeeled

4 cups milk

**bouquet garni (a bay leaf and green
  herbs tied together or in a tea ball)**

3 tablespoons of butter

115g/4oz salt pork, diced

salt and pepper

36 fresh shucked oysters, juice reserved

chopped parsley to garnish

METHOD

1. Cook the potatoes in boiling salted water until just
tender. Meanwhile, bring the milk to a boil, remove
from heat, dunk in the bouquet garn, and allow to
infuse. Then sauté the diced salt pork in a little
butter over low heat until it is just cooked through.

2. When the potatoes are done, peel and mash, then
whip in the hot herbed milk. Add the salt pork drained
of their grease. Season to taste. Bring to a boil, stirring
constantly, then add the oysters with their liquid.
Simmer for a few minutes. Taste for seasoning and stir
in the rest of the butter. You can make a nice
presentation from a tureen at the table or just ladle
into bowls in the kitchen and serve at once, garnished
with chopped parsley.

Serves 6–8 people.

Manhattan Oyster Chowder

INGREDIENTS

2 tablespoons olive oil

1 onion, chopped into bite-sized chunks

125g/4^1/$_2$oz dark-gilled mushrooms, quartered

2 cloves garlic, chopped

3 cups/750mL fish stock

455g/16oz can of tomatoes, seeded and chopped

bay leaf

^{1}/$_4$ teaspoon rosemary, crushed to a powder

^{1}/$_4$ teaspoon oregano, crushed to a powder

pinch hot pepper flakes

1 zucchini, cut into bite-sized chunks

1 jar standard oysters

parsley

METHOD

1. Heat oil in large saucepan and sauté the onions and mushrooms, until the onions are golden and the mushrooms are brown. Add garlic and stir for a minute. Add fish stock, chopped tomatoes and the juice reserved from the can of tomatoes. Stir in the bay leaf, rosemary, oregano, and hot pepper flashes. Bring to a boil, then reduce heat and simmer, partially covered, for 25 minutes.

2. Add zucchini, cover and simmer another 10 minutes, until the zucchini is almost tender. Slip the oysters with their liquid into the soup and cook, uncovered, just until the edges of the oysters begin to curl. (You want them tender, not chewy.)

3. Ladle into bowls. Sprinkle with parsley and serve immediately. Fat, dense oyster biscuits taste very good with this soup.

Serves 4

Note: This spicy and chunky chowder is just the thing for a warming lunch or a light dinner with lots of side dishes; serve hot to 6.

Oyster and Brie Soup

INGREDIENTS

3 dozen small to medium
  oysters in their liquor
4 cups cold water
85g/4oz unsalted butter
1/4 to 1/2 cup flour
1 cup onion coarsely chopped
1/2 rib celery coarsely chopped
1/2 teaspoon white pepper
1/2 teaspoon ground red pepper
500g/18oz brie cheese cut in small pieces
2 cups double cream
1/2 bunch green onions chopped
1/2 cup champagne
1 handful cured smoked ham
  finely chopped
250g/9oz bacon, fried and crumbled

METHOD

1. Combine oysters and water and refrigerate for 1 hour.

2. Strain the oysters and reserve the water. In a large skillet, melt the butter over low heat. Add the flour and whisk until smooth. Add the onions and celery and sauté about 3 minutes, stirring occasionally.

3. Stir in the peppers and sauté 2 minutes and set aside. In a large saucepan, bring the oyster water to a boil. Stir vegetable mixture. Turn heat to high. Add cheese; cook for 2 minutes, stirring constantly, until cheese starts to melt. Lower heat to a simmer and continue cooking for about 4 minutes, stirring constantly.

4. Remove from heat, strain soup and return to pot. Turn heat to high and cook 1 minute, stirring constantly. Stir in cream, cook until close to a boil (about 2 minutes). Add green onions and champagne if desired.

5. Lower heat and add the oysters and handful of cured smoked ham. Check the seasoning at this point and add red pepper and salt to taste. When oysters curl, serve immediately in bread bowls with crumbled bacon to garnish the top.

Serves 4

Oyster Cream Soup with Lemony Carrots

INGREDIENTS

2 whole carrots, peeled

2 tablespoons lemon juice

1 tablespoon olive oil

2 tablespoons butter

2 medium onion, chopped

1 bunch green onions, chopped

3 garlic cloves, chopped

4 canned tomatoes (or 2 fresh), peeled, seeded, and chopped

1 teaspoon basil, chopped (or pesto)

1 teaspoon thyme

salt and white pepper

cayenne pepper

5 cups milk

1 cup/250mL/9fl oz whipping cream

570g/20oz oysters

METHOD

1. Boil the carrots until tender. Drain, slice thinly and mix with lemon juice and oil. Refrigerate.

2. Melt the butter in a large saucepan over medium-low heat. Add onions and garlic and cook until translucent (about 10 minutes). Add the tomatoes, increase heat and cook for 10 minutes or until thickened, stirring occasionally. Stir in the basil and thyme, salt, pepper, and cayenne to taste. Cook until all the moisture has evaporated, then purée in a blender or food processor. At this point, you can refrigerate until ready to serve.

3. When ready to eat, stir the onion mixture into a saucepan with the milk and cream and bring to a boil. Reduce heat, season, and add the carrots with marinade. Add the whole jar of oysters, including the liquid, and poach for 2 minutes or until just opaque.

4. Ladle into flat soup bowls and garnish with the basil leaves or swirl a teaspoon of pesto through each bowl.

Serves 6

Note: A thick, tangy soup to serve as a warming lunch or light supper with lots of bread and salad; serve hot to 6 people.

Hot and Sour Scallop Soup

INGREDIENTS

4 cups canned low sodium chicken broth

1 cup mushrooms, thinly sliced

$1/4$ cup bamboo shoots, sliced

$1/2$lb sea or bay scallops, sliced 5mm/$1/4$-inch thick

1 teaspoon low sodium soy sauce

$1/4$ teaspoon white pepper

2 tablespoons cornstarch

3 tablespoons warm, water

1 egg, beaten

3 tablespoons rice vinegar (2 tablespoons white wine vinegar may be substituted)

$1/3$ cup thinly sliced green onions

METHOD

1. Place chicken broth, mushrooms and bamboo shoots in saucepan. Bring to the boil, reduce heat and simmer 5 minutes. Rinse scallops under cold running water. Add scallops, soy sauce and pepper.

2. Bring to the boil. Mix the cornflour with warm water. Add cornflour mixture and stir a few seconds until thickened. Stir briskly with a chopstick and gradually pour in egg. Remove from heat. Stir in vinegar and sprinkle with green onion. Serve immediately.

Serves 4

Oyster Hots

INGREDIENTS

6 cups fish stock

2 potatoes, cut into a fine julienne

2 carrots, cut into a fine julienne

1/2 red capsicum, cut into a fine julienne

1/2 to 1 jalapeno pepper, cut into fine slivers

1/2 teaspoon grated lemon zest

1/4 teaspoon thyme

salt and white pepper

1 jar standard oysters

juice of 1 lemon (2–3 tablespoons)

paper thin rounds of lemon, sprinkled with thyme to garnish

METHOD

1. Bring the stock to a the boil in a large saucepan. Add potatoes, carrots, red capsicum, jalapeno slivers, lemon zest, thyme and salt and pepper to taste. Reduce heat, leave uncovered and simmer for 15 minutes or until the vegetables are tender.

2. Slip the oysters with their liquid into the simmering stock and cook for 2 minutes just until their edges curl. Remove from heat, stir in lemon juice, and adjust for seasoning. Ladle into bowls, top each with a lemon slice and sprinkling of thyme. Serve immediately.

Serves 4–6

Note: So clean and piquant, you'll think you've been to the beach; serve hot to 4-6 people as a stimulating first course.

Turmeric-Infused Scallop Soup

INGREDIENTS

2 tablespoons unsalted butter

$1/2$ teaspoon turmeric

3 shallots, finely chopped

1 bottle dry white wine

4 cups fish stock

$1/2$ cup/125mL/$4^{1}/_{2}$fl oz crème fraiche

3 $1/2$ cups double cream

freshly ground white pepper

$1/2$ teaspoon white wine vinegar

METHOD

1. In a large saucepan coat butter, tumeric, scallops and shallots over moderately low heat, stirring until shallots are softened. Add wine and stock and simmer mixture until reduced by half. Take off heat and allow to cool.

2. Pour soup into a blender, and blend until smooth. Put back onto heat in a saucepan, add crème fraiche and double cream and simmer, stirring occasionally for 15 minutes.

3. Pour soup through a fine sieve into a heatproof bowl. Stir in white-pepper, vinegar and salt to taste. In another bowl whisk remaining $1/2$ cup double cream until thickened and stir into soup until incorporated. Serve with wedge of herbed flatbread.

Serves 10

Rich Scallop Soup

INGREDIENTS

2 cups/500mL/18fl oz milk
1 cup/250mL/9fl oz double cream
2 tablespoons butter or margarine
1 teaspoon salt
$^{1}/_{4}$ teaspoon white pepper
1 teaspoon Worcestershire sauce
500g/18oz scallops, chopped into
small pieces
paprika
3 tablespoon parsley, fresh, finely
chopped

METHOD

1. In the top of a double boiler, blend milk, cream, butter or margarine, salt, pepper and Worcestershire sauce. Fill the bottom with boiling water and bring to a simmer, stirring frequently. Add scallops to the mixture and cook until tender about 8–10 minutes. Pour hot soup into individual bowls. Sprinkle each bowl with paprika and parsley.

Serves 6

SCALLOP &
OYSTER SALADS

Barbecued Seafood Salad

INGREDIENTS

2 tablespoons lemon juice

1 tablespoon olive oil

300g/10½oz firm white fish (such as swordfish, mackerel, blue-eye cod or barramundi), cut into 3 cm cubes

300g/10½oz pink fish (such as salmon, ocean trout, marlin or tuna)

12 scallops

12 uncooked prawns (with or without shell)

1 calamari (squid), cleaned and tube cut into rings, (discard the tentacles or freeze) tentacles for another use

1 bunch/250g/9oz watercress, broken into sprigs

1 large red onion, cut into rings

1 telegraph cucumber, sliced thinly

Raspberry and Tarragon Dressing

3 tablespoons fresh tarragon, chopped

2 tablespoons raspberry or red wine vinegar

2 tablespoons lemon juice

1 tablespoon olive oil

freshly ground black pepper

METHOD

1. Place lemon juice and oil in a bowl. Whisk to combine. Add white and pink fish, scallops, prawns and calamari. Toss to combine. Cover and marinate in the refrigerator for 1 hour or until ready to use (do not marinate for longer than 2 hours).

2. For the dressing, place tarragon, vinegar, lemon juice, oil and black pepper to taste in a screwtop jar. Shake to combine and set aside.

3. Preheat a barbecue or char-grill pan until very hot. Line a serving platter with watercress.

4. Drain seafood mixture. Place on barbecue plate or in pan. Add onion and cook, turning several times, for 6–8 minutes or until seafood is just cooked. Take care not to overcook or the seafood will be tough and dry.

5. Transfer seafood mixture to a bowl. Add cucumber and dressing. Toss to combine. Spoon seafood mixture over watercress. Serve immediately.

Serves 8

BARBECUED SEAFOOD SALAD

Oyster Salad

INGREDIENTS

24 oysters, on the half shell or meat only

2 tomatoes, sliced thinly

lettuce

6 teaspoons lemon juice

1 cup celery, diced

mayonnaise

paprika

METHOD

1. Cook oysters in their own juice until the edges curl up. Drain and chill.

2. Place a lettuce leaf on 4 salad plates. Shred rest of lettuce and place on lettuce leaves.

3. Lay 6 oysters on each lettuce leaf and sprinkle with lemon juice.

4. Place tomato and celery on top. Dab oysters with mayonnaise, sprinkle with paprika, and chill for 1 hour before serving.

Serves 4

Note: If your Oysters are have no oyster shell, just place each oyster meat on the baking dish to cook.

Spinach Salad with Scallops

INGREDIENTS

500g/18oz fresh scallops

$1/2$ cup orange juice

$1/2$ cup dry white wine

$1/2$ teaspoon salt

250g/18oz baby spinach leaves, washed and crisped

2 medium sized oranges, segmented

Dressing

$1/4$ cup orange juice

2 teaspoon finely chopped parsley

$1/3$ cup olive oil

1 teaspoon balsamic vinegar

$1/2$ teaspoon sugar

pinch of salt

METHOD

1. Remove any brown membrane from the scallops, rinse well. Detach the coral and separate

2. Heat orange juice, wine and salt to simmering point, add white scallops and poach for 2 minutes. Add the coral and poach 1 minute more. Do not overcook. Remove to a bowl with the juice and refrigerate to cool. Drain the scallops before inclusion in the salad.

3. Toss the spinach, orange segments and drained scallops quickly together. Combine dressing ingredients in a screw top jar, shake well, and toss through the salad. Serve in individual entire dishes.

Serves 4

Tips: To crisp the spinach, place the washed spinach in a clean towel and refrigerate for 1 hour

Tips: To segment the orange. Peel the orange t king off all of the pith. With a small sharp knife cut between the membrane line to remove each segment.

Scallop and Bacon Salad

INGREDIENTS

a few good handfuls endive
1 cucumber, diced
cherry tomatoes, quartered
olive oil
juice of 1 lemon or lime
vinegar
salt and pepper
3 rashers streaky bacon
8 scallops, shells removed

METHOD

1. Mix the salad of endive, cucumber, and tomatoes in a large bowl, and dress with a little oil, half the lemon juice and vinegar and season with salt and pepper.

2. Fry the bacon in a little olive oil on a low heat, until crispy. Remove and set aside on some kitchen paper.

3. Fry the scallops in the bacon fat for only a few minutes on each side. They should adopt a lovely golden colour. Season lightly, and squeeze in the remaining lemon juice. Remove from heat.

4. Put a some salad on a plate and place a few scallops on top. Break up the bacon and scatter the pieces over. Pour over some of the juices from the pan and serve.

Serves 2

Note: For a bit of a twist you could serve small portions of this in the scallop shells.

Salad of Scallops on Bitter Greens with Strawberries

INGREDIENTS

1 granny smith apple, unpeeled, in very small
  cubes or slices (squeeze a lemon over to
  prevent browning)

about 20 small strawberries washed and halved

3 tablespoon of liver oil

salad greens – enough lambs tongue, iceberg,
  rocket, mizuna, chicory or yellow section of
  curly endive leaves to make a mound and
  cover the base of 6 entrée plates (use any
  leafy mixture you fancy)

olive oil

500g/18oz scallops

Vinaigrette

12 tablespoons olive oil

3 tablespoons raspberry vinegar

salt and pepper

2 tablespoons chopped chives, finely cut

METHOD

1. Place scallops in a bowl with the oil and marinate for 1 hour. Divide salad greens amongst the plates.

2. Shake vinaigrette ingredients together in a jar.

3. Add olive oil to a heavy-based wok or fry pan and on medium to high heat, quickly stir-fry scallops for 30 seconds or until seared very light brown, about 30 seconds but don't crowd them or they will stew.

4. Spoon scallops over salad greens, scatter strawberries and apple cubes all over, shake vinaigrette and drizzle over the top.

5. Sprinkle with chives and serve immediately.

Serves 4–6

Note: Other berries, such as raspberries, can be used when in season.

Scallop and Watercress Salad

INGREDIENTS

Dressing

2/3cup/170mL/5fl oz walnut oil
  or olive oil

2 tablespoons red wine vinegar

2 small cloves garlic, minced

salt

white pepper

10 fresh scallops

3 cups watercress, discard woody stems,
  select tender tips only

1 cup water chestnuts, halved

1/2 cup cherry tomatoes

1/2 cup walnut halves

1 cup bean sprouts, topped and tailed

METHOD

1. Mix the dressing ingredients together in a
jar and shake well.

2. Place the scallops on a plate suitable for
steaming. Sprinkle the scallops with a little of
the dressing and steam gently over boiling
water for 6 minutes.

3. Wash and dry the watercress, and snap into
12cm/5in sections. In a serving bowl, combine
the watercress, water chestnuts, cherry
tomatoes, walnuts and bean sprouts. Pour on
the dressing and toss through the salad.
Gently mix in the scallops.

Serves 4

Grilled Sea Scallops and Pink-Grapefruit Salad

INGREDIENTS

455–680g/1–1^1/$_2$ lb sea scallops

2 large pink grapefruits, peeled and
   segmented (squeeze and reserve juice)

1 cup/250ml/9fl oz non-fat plain yoghurt

1 tablespoon honey

^{1}/$_3$ cup couscous, cooked and fluffed

1 bag mixed baby lettuce leaves

1 large tomato, cored and diced

15g/5oz baby green beans, cleaned and
cooked

^{1}/$_4$ package radish sprouts

fresh cracked black pepper to taste

METHOD

1. Season and grill scallops. Set aside and allow to cool. In a mixing bowl, combine grapefruit juice, yoghurt, and honey.

2. Spoon couscous into base of salad bowl. Arrange mixed baby lettuce leaves in the center, top with sea scallops, pink grapfruit segments, green beans, tomato, and radish sprouts. Season with fresh black cracked pepper.

Serves 4

GRILLED SEA SCALLOPS AND PINK GRAPEFRUIT SALAD

SAUTÉED SCALLOPS WITH FETA

Sautéed Scallops with Feta

INGREDIENTS

$1/2$ large onion

$1^1/2$ red capsicum

2 jalepeno peppers, sliced

500g/18oz large sea scallops

55g/2oz butter

$1/2$ cup/125mL/$4^1/2$fl oz white wine

$1/2$ cup mozzarella cheese

$1/2$ cup feta cheese

pinch garlic to taste

salt to taste

METHOD

1. Sauté onion, capsicum, jalepenos and sea scallops in butter until soft.

2. Add white wine and cover for 45 seconds. Sprinkle with mozzarella and feta. Add pinches of garlic, salt and chilli powder and let simmer until cheeses melt. Serve over rice.

Serves 2

Scallops, Mussels, and Asparagus Salad

INGREDIENTS

250g/8oz fresh or frozen sea scallops

6 large or 12 small fresh mussels in shells

1 cup/250mL/8fl oz water

250g/8oz fresh asparagus spears

$1/3$ cup/85mL/$2^1/2$ fl oz light sour cream

$1/2$ teaspoon finely shredded lime peel

2 teaspoons lime juice

2 teaspoons salmon roe or red caviar

$1/8$ teaspoon pepper

1 head butterhead lettuce

fresh chives

lime wedges

METHOD

1. Thaw scallops, if frozen. Scrub mussels under cold running water; remove beards and discard. Soak the mussels in cold salted water for 15 minutes, then drain and rinse. Repeat soaking, draining, and rinsing twice more. Set aside.

2. In a large saucepan bring the 1 cup water just to boiling. Place asparagus in saucepan and cook, covered, about 3 minutes or until crisp-tender. Do not overcook. Remove asparagus, reserving water in saucepan. Rinse asparagus in cold water then cover and chill in the refrigerator. Meanwhile, return water to just boiling. Add mussels to water and simmer, covered, for 5 minutes or until shells open. (Discard any mussels that do not open.) Drain and rinse mussels then cover and chill in the refrigerator for at least 2 hours.

3. Heat oil in non stick skillet. Cook scallops in hot oil for 1–3 minutes or until scallops are opaque. Remove scallops and cover and chill in the refrigerator for at least 2 hours. In a small bowl, combine sour cream, lime peel, lime juice, half the roe or caviar, and the pepper. Cover and chill in the refrigerator.

4. Arrange chilled mussels, scallops, and asparagus on lettuce leaves. Serve with sour cream mixture and remaining roe or caviar. Garnish salad with chives and lime wedges.

Serves 2

Seared Scallop Salad

INGREDIENTS

2 teaspoons sesame oil

2 cloves garlic, crushed

340g/12oz scallops, cleaned

4 rashers bacon, chopped

1 cos lettuce, leaves separated

55g/2oz croûtons

fresh Parmesan cheese

Mustard Dressing

3 tablespoons mayonnaise

1 tablespoon olive oil

1 tablespoon vinegar

2 teaspoons Dijon mustard

METHOD

1. To make dressing, place mayonnaise, olive oil, vinegar and mustard in a bowl, mix to combine and set aside.

2. Heat sesame oil in a frying pan over a high heat, add garlic and scallops and cook, stirring, for 1 minute or until scallops just turn opaque. Remove scallop mixture from pan and set aside. Add bacon to pan and cook, stirring, for 4 minutes or until crisp. Remove bacon from pan and drain on absorbent kitchen paper.

3. Place lettuce leaves in a large salad bowl, add dressing and toss to coat. Add bacon, croûtons and shavings of Parmesan cheese and toss to combine. Spoon scallop mixture over salad and serve.

Serves 4

Scallop Salad with Fruit Salsa

INGREDIENTS

1 small pineapple (about 1^{1}/3kg/3lb)

1 cup strawberries, chopped

^{3}/4 cup peach, pitted, peeled, and chopped or chopped frozen unsweetened peach slices

2 jalapeno peppers, seeded and chopped (2 tablespoons)

1–2 tablespoons, chopped fresh coriander or parsley

several dashes bottled hot pepper sauce

^{1}/4 cup orange juice

340g/12oz fresh or frozen sea scallops or bay scallops

1 teaspoon salt

cos lettuce leaves

kiwifruit (optional) peeled, sliced

coriander leaves (optional)

METHOD

1. Using a sharp knife cut two 2cm/3/4in thick slices from the center of the pineapple. Cut each slice into six wedges. Remove the hard core from each wedge. Wrap and refrigerate the pineapple wedges. Peel, core, and finely chop enough of the remaining pineapple to make ^{3}/4 cup (save the remaining pineapple for another use).

2. For salsa, combine the ^{3}/4 cup chopped pineapple, strawberries, peach, jalapeno peppers, coriander, and hot pepper sauce. Place about 1 cup of the fruit mixture into a blender or food processor with orange juice. Cover and blend or process just till pureed. Stir into remaining fruit mixture. Cover and chill for several hours or overnight, stirring occasionally.

3. Thaw scallops, if frozen. Cut large scallops in half. Bring 4 cups salted water to the boil. Add scallops. Simmer, uncovered, for 1–2 minutes, stirring occasionally or until scallops are opaque. Drain, and rinse under cold running water. Cover; chill for several hours or overnight.

4. To serve, line 4 salad plates with lettuce leaves. Arrange three of the reserved pineapple wedges on each plate, with the point of the wedge toward the center. Divide scallops among the plates. Top with salsa. If desired, garnish each plate with sliced kiwifruit and coriander leaves.

Serves 4

Squid and Scallop Salad

INGREDIENTS

1 red capsicum, seeded and halved
1 yellow or green capsicum, seeded and halved
2 squid (calamari) tubes
250g/9oz scallops, roe (coral) removed
250g/9oz asparagus, cut into 5cm/2in pieces, blanched
1 red onion, sliced
3 tablespoons fresh coriander leaves
1 bunch rocket or watercress

Herb and Balsamic Dressing

1 tablespoon fresh ginger, finely grated
1 tablespoon chopped fresh rosemary
1 clove garlic, crushed
1/4 cup olive oil
2 tablespoons lime juice
1 tablespoon balsamic or red wine vinegar

METHOD

1. To make dressing, place ginger, rosemary, garlic, oil, lime juice and vinegar in a screwtop jar and shake well to combine. Set aside.

2. Preheat barbecue to a high heat. Place red and yellow or green capsicum halves, skin side down on lightly oiled barbecue grill and cook for 5–10 minutes or until skins are blistered and charred. Place capsicum in a plastic food bag or paper bag and set aside until cool enough to handle. Remove skins from capsicum and cut flesh into thin strips.

3. Cut squid (calamari) tubes lengthwise and open out flat. Using a sharp knife cut parallel lines down the length of the squid, taking care not to cut through the flesh. Make more cuts in the opposite direction to form a diamond pattern. Cut into 5cm/2in squares.

4. Place squid and scallops on lightly oiled barbecue plate (griddle) and cook, turning several times, for 3 minutes or until tender. Set aside to cool slightly.

5. Combine red and yellow or green capsicum, asparagus, onion and coriander. Line a large serving platter with rocket or watercress, top with vegetables, squid and scallops. Drizzle with dressing and serve immediately.

Serves 4

Warm Seafood Salad

INGREDIENTS

500g/18oz assorted salad leaves

250g/9oz yellow teardrop tomatoes (optional)

250g/9oz cherry tomatoes, halved

2 avocados, stoned, peeled and sliced

145g/5oz snow peas (mangetout), trimmed and blanched

250g/9oz asparagus spears, cut into 5cm/2in pieces, blanched

3 calamari (squid) tubes

30g/1oz butter

250g/9oz scallops

16 uncooked medium prawns, shelled and deveined, tails left intact

200g/7oz thickly sliced smoked ocean trout or smoked salmon

Oriental Dressing

1 tablespoon rice vinegar

1 tablespoon fish sauce

2 tablespoons sweet chilli sauce

1 tablespoon fresh basil, shredded

1 tablespoon lemon juice

1/4 cup water

Note: This salad is great served warm, but also may be made ahead of time and served chilled. If serving chilled, prepare the salad, seafood and dressing and store separately in the refrigerator. Just prior to serving, assemble the salad as described in the recipe.

METHOD

1. Arrange salad leaves, teardrop tomatoes (if using) and cherry tomatoes, avocados, snow peas (mangetout) and asparagus on a large serving platter.

2. To make dressing, place vinegar, fish sauce, chilli sauce, basil, lemon juice and water in a small bowl and whisk to combine.

3. Cut calamari (squid) tubes, lengthwise, and open out flat. Using a sharp knife, cut parallel lines down the length of the calamari taking care not to cut right through the flesh. Make more cuts in the opposite direction to form a diamond pattern. Cut each piece into 5cm/2in squares.

4. Melt butter in a large frying pan, add scallops and prawns and stir-fry for 3 minutes. Add calamari pieces and stir-fry for 1 minute longer. Arrange cooked seafood and smoked ocean trout or smoked salmon on salad and drizzle with dressing.

Serves 8

MAIN MEALS

Chicken and Oyster Casserole

INGREDIENTS

1kg/2¼ lb chicken thighs, skinned and boned

55g/2oz plain flour

salt and black pepper

2 onions, finely chopped

4 cloves of garlic, crushed

225g/9oz mushrooms

1 tablespoon chopped fresh sage

170mL/6fl oz white wine

170mL/6fl oz water

zest and juice of one lemon

145mL/5fl oz double cream

18 oysters

METHOD

1. Toss the chicken in the flour, salt and black pepper and seal in a frying pan, a couple of pieces at a time. Remove to a large casserole. Fry the onions to soften then add the garlic, mushrooms and sage. Add to the chicken. Deglaze the pan with the white wine and add it, with the water and lemon juice and zest, to the casserole.

2. Cover and bake in the oven, for 1 ½ hours at 180°C/350°F. Remove from the oven, add the cream and oysters and return to the oven for 15 minutes. Allow to rest for 10 minutes before giving it one last stir and serving. It should have thickened with the flour, but if it didn't, add a little cornflour slaked with milk as you remove it from the oven

Serves 4

Baked Oysters with Bacon

INGREDIENTS

1 clove garlic, crushed

45g/1½ oz butter

115g/4oz fresh breadcrumbs

salt and pepper to taste

24 oysters (bottled or fresh)

3 bacon rashers

METHOD

1. Preheat oven to 210°C/410°F.

2. Sauté garlic in butter 1–2 minutes. Add breadcrumbs, salt and pepper, and fry until just turning brown.

3. Drain oysters, and place in a shallow, greased ovenproof dish.

4. Cover all over with browned crumbs, and place strips of bacon over top.

5. Put in hot oven until bacon is browned and crisp.

Serves 4

Coconut Prawns and Scallops

INGREDIENTS

1kg/2^{1}/$_4$lb large uncooked prawns, shelled and deveined, tails left intact

3 egg whites, lightly beaten

85g/3oz shredded coconut

vegetable oil for deep-frying

1 tablespoon peanut oil

4 fresh red chillies, seeded and sliced

2 small fresh green chillies, seeded and sliced

2 cloves garlic, crushed

1 tablespoon fresh ginger, shredded

3 kaffir lime leaves, finely shredded

340g/12oz scallops

115g/4oz snow peas leaves
   or sprouts

2 tablespoons palm or brown sugar

^{1}/$_4$ cup lime juice

2 tablespoons Thai fish sauce (nam pla)

METHOD

1. Dip prawns in egg white, then roll in coconut to coat. Heat vegetable oil in a large saucepan until a cube of bread dropped in browns in 50 seconds. Cook prawns, a few at a time, for 2 – 3 minutes or until golden and crisp. Drain on absorbent paper and keep warm.

2. Heat peanut oil in a wok over a high heat, add red and green chillies, garlic, ginger and lime leaves and stir-fry for 2 – 3 minutes or until fragrant.

3. Add scallops to wok and stir-fry for 3 minutes or until opaque. Add cooked prawns, snow pea leaves, sugar, lime juice and fish sauce and stir-fry for 2 minutes or until heated.

Serves 6

Curried Scallops with Water Chestnuts

INGREDIENTS

2 tablespoons light salad oil

1 small onion, chopped

2 tablespoons minced fresh ginger root

2 cloves minced garlic

1 teaspoon curry powder

1/2 teaspoon ground coriander

1/2 teaspoon crushed red hot chilli

340g/12oz sea scallops, rinsed and cut
crosswise into 5mm/1/4in slices

225g/8oz fresh water chestnuts, ends
trimmed and sliced or you can use
canned water chestnuts

2 tablespoons fresh coriander

1/2 cup chicken broth

1 teaspoon cornflour

1 teaspoon fish sauce, or soy sauce

1/2 teaspoon cider vinegar

METHOD

1. Place a medium sized frying pan over
medium high heat. Add oil, onion, ginger and
garlic. Stir often until onion is tinged with
brown (about 10 minutes). Add curry,
coriander and chillies and stir until curry
becomes fragrant (about 1 minute).

2. Add scallops and water chestnuts and gently
stir for 2 minutes until scallops are almost
opaque throughout (cut to test), for 2 minutes.
Add sauce mixture, and stir until it thickens.
Pour onto a plate and sprinkle with coriander.

3. For sauce mixture: Combine chicken broth,
cornflour, fish or soy sauce, and cider vinegar.

Serves 2

Ginger Scallop Stir-Fry

INGREDIENTS

2 tablespoons fresh lime juice

2 tablespoons rice wine

1 clove garlic, crushed

225g/8oz bay scallops

1 tablespoon sesame oil

2 teaspoon ginger, finely grated

4 spring onions, cut diagonally into

1cm/1/2in lengths

85g/3oz button mushrooms, sliced

1/2 red capsicum, diced

2 teaspoons soy sauce

pepper

1 teaspoon cornflour

2 tablespoons water

METHOD

1. Combine the lime juice with the rice wine and crushed garlic. Marinate the scallops for 15 minutes. Set aside. Heat the sesame oil in a hot wok or large skillet until almost smoking.

2. To the wok, add the ginger, spring onions, mushrooms and red capsicum. Stir-fry for about 3 minutes, until the ginger has become fragrant. Add the scallops and marinade.

3. Continue stir-frying for another 3 minutes, until scallops have become opaque. Add the soy sauce and mix thoroughly. Add pepper to taste.

4. Make a slurry of the cornflour and water. Drizzle the slurry into the wok. Cook for another minute or two or until the sauce has thickened and become smooth. Serve immediately with steamed white rice.

Serves 4

Coquilles Saint-Jacques en Seviche
(Scallops Marinated in Citrus Juices)

INGREDIENTS

500g/18oz sea or bay scallops

juice of 2 limes

juice of 1 orange

grated rind of 1 lemon,

1 lime, ¹/₂ orange

salt and freshly cracked pepper to taste

2 tablespoons orange liquer

4–6 lime slices

METHOD

1. Slice the raw scallops thinly. Mix all ingredients, except the lettuce and add the scallops. Let sit covered in the refrigerator overnight. (The acid in the citrus juice will cook the scallops.)

2. To serve, arrange your favourite lettuce on cold plates, and top with a mound of the scallops.

3. Garnish with a slice of lime. This recipe should be made one day prior to serving

Serves 4–6

Baked Oysters

INGREDIENTS

40g/1¹/₂oz butter

200g/7oz fresh breadcrumbs

1 teaspoon freshly crushed garlic

1 tablespoon fresh chopped parsley

2 dozen fresh oysters

65g/2¹/₂oz Parmesan cheese (freshly grated)

30g/1oz butter (extra)

METHOD

1. Preheat oven to 210°C/410°F.

2. Grease an ovenproof platter (just large enough to hold the oysters in a single layer).

3. Melt butter in a frypan over a moderate heat. When the foam subsides, add the breadcrumbs and garlic and toss (until golden). Stir in the parsley.

4. Spread about two-thirds of the breadcrumb mixture in the bottom of the platter and arrange the oysters over it.

5. Mix the rest of the breadcrumbs with the grated cheese and spread over the oysters.

6. Dot the top with the extra butter chopped into tiny pieces.

7. Bake in the preheated hot oven for 15 minutes (or until top is golden).

Serves 6–8

Ginger Scallops

INGREDIENTS

1 tablespoon peanut oil

2 teaspoons minced fresh ginger root

1 clove minced garlic

1^1/$_2$ cups whole snow pea pods, fresh
or frozen

1 cup carrot, thinly sliced

455g/1lb sea scallops, roe removed

1 tablespoon light soy sauce

^{1}/$_8$ teaspoon salt

2 teaspoons cornflour

^{1}/$_4$ cup sliced spring onions

2 cups hot cooked rice

METHOD

1. Heat oil in wok over medium-high heat and add ginger and garlic. Stir-fry for 30 seconds. Add snow peas and carrots and stir-fry a couple of minutes.

2. Remove vegetables from wok, set aside and keep warm. Add scallops to wok and cook over medium-high heat about 3 minutes, or until scallops are cooked, stirring constantly.

3. Combine soy sauce, salt and cornflour, stir well and add to the wok. Add spring onions and cook 1 minute, stirring constantly. Add vegetables and serve over hot rice.

Serves 4

Griddled Scallops with Orange Salsa

INGREDIENTS

2 small oranges

4 sun-dried tomatoes in oil,
    drained and chopped

1 clove garlic, crushed

1 tablespoon balsamic vinegar

4 tablespoons extra virgin olive oil

salt and black pepper

1 large head fennel, cut lengthways into 8

slices

12 fresh prepared scallops

4 tablespoons crème fraiche

rocket leaves to serve

METHOD

1. Slice the top and bottom off one of the oranges, then cut away the peel and pith, following the curve of the fruit. Cut between the membranes to release the segments, then chop roughly. Squeeze the juice of the other orange into a bowl, add the chopped orange, tomatoes, garlic, vinegar and 3 tablespoons of the oil, then season.

2. Heat a ridged cast-iron grill pan or heavy-based frying pan. Brush both sides of each fennel slice with half the remaining oil. Cook for 2—3 minutes on each side, until tender and charred. Transfer to serving plates and keep warm.

3. Brush the scallops with the remaining oil and cook for 1 minute, then turn and cook for 30 seconds or until cooked through. Top the fennel with 1 tablespoon of crème fraiche, 3 scallops and the salsa. Serve with the rocket.

Serves 4

Creamed Oysters

INGREDIENTS

1 large bottle oysters

2 tablespoons butter

2 tablespoons plain flour

1 cup milk

65mL/2^{1}/4fl oz cream

pinch cayenne pepper

2 tablespoons dry sherry

salt to taste

4 slices hot, buttered toast

chopped parsley, to garnish

METHOD

1. Drain oysters (reserving ^{1}/4 cup liquid).

2. Melt butter in saucepan, stir in flour, and cook (for 2 minutes) over low heat.

3. Slowly stir in milk, cream and reserved oyster liquid. Add cayenne pepper, sherry and salt (to taste). Simmer for 2 minutes.

4. Add oysters, and simmer another minute or two (until oysters are just plump).

5. Spoon over toast and sprinkle with parsley.

Serves 4

GRIDDLED SCALLOPS WITH ORANGE SALSA

Scallop and Mango Sangchssajang

INGREDIENTS

600g/21oz scallops

1 tablespoon cornflour

2 teaspoons brown sugar

2 teaspoons olive or peanut (groundnut) oil

2 shallots, thinly sliced

1 tablespoon fresh ginger, grated

6 spears fresh asparagus, chopped

1/2 cup rice wine (mirin) or dry white wine

2 tablespoons lime or lemon juice

2 teaspoons fish sauce, optional

2 teaspoons reduced-salt soy sauce

few drops chilli sauce or 1 small fresh red chilli, thinly sliced

1 mango, flesh diced

2 tablespoons fresh sweet basil or coriander, shredded

370g/13oz hot cooked jasmine or calrose rice

1 butter lettuce or radicchio, leaves separated

METHOD

1. Place scallops, cornflour and sugar in a plastic food bag. Toss gently to coat.

2. Heat 1 teaspoon of the oil in a non-stick frying pan over a high heat. Add scallops. Stir-fry for 2—3 minutes or until scallops are just cooked. Remove scallops from pan. Set aside.

3. Heat remaining oil in pan. Add shallots and ginger.

4. Stir-fry for 1 minute or until soft. Add asparagus, wine, lime juice and fish, soy and chilli sauces. Stir-fry for 4 minutes or until the asparagus is tender. Add mango and basil. Toss to combine.

5. To serve, spoon rice into lettuce cups, then spoon in some of the scallop mixture. To eat, fold lettuce around scallops and eat in your hands.

Serves 4 as a light meal or 6 as a starter

Pasta with Scallops, Zucchini, and Tomatoes

INGREDIENTS

455g/1lb dry fettucine pasta

1/4 cup olive oil

3 cloves garlic, minced

2 zucchinis, diced

1/2 teaspoon salt

1/2 teaspoon crushed red pepper flakes

4 Roma tomatoes, chopped

1 cup chopped fresh basil, optional

455g/1lb bay scallops

2 tablespoons grated Parmesan cheese

METHOD

1. Cook pasta in a large pot with boiling salted water until al dente. Drain.

2. Meanwhile, heat oil in a large skillet, add garlic and cook until tender. Add the zucchini, salt, red pepper flakes, and sauté for 10 minutes. Add chopped tomatoes, bay scallops, and fresh basil (if using) and simmer for 5 minutes, or until scallops are opaque.

3. Pour sauce over cooked pasta and serve with grated Parmesan cheese.

Serves 4—6

Scallops with Vegetables

INGREDIENTS

1 teaspoon cornflour

1 tablespoon water

1 teaspoon soy sauce

1/2 teaspoon sugar

100g/3 1/2oz green beans

1 tablespoon oil

250g/9oz scallops

1 white onion (thinly sliced)

115g/4oz mushrooms (sliced)

115g/4oz celery (sliced)

55g/2oz bamboo shoots (thinly sliced)

**115g/4oz canned pineapple pieces
  (drained)**

1 cup chicken stock

METHOD

1. Mix together cornflour, water, soy sauce and sugar.

2. Drop beans into boiling water, and cook for 3–4 minutes.

3. Heat about 1 tablespoon oil, and add scallops. Fry for 1 minute, stirring constantly. Remove scallops from pan.

4. Add onion, mushrooms, celery and bamboo shoots. Stir-fry for another 3 minutes. Add pineapple pieces, stock and beans. Cook over medium heat for 2 minutes.

5. Add scallops. Stir the cornflour mixture, add to pan, and cook, stirring, for 2 minutes.

Serves 4

Pasta with Pesto and Scallops

INGREDIENTS

500g/18oz dry fettucine pasta

1/4 cup pesto sauce

2 tablespoons olive oil

3 tablespoons olive oil, extra

1/2 onion, chopped

2 cloves garlic, minced

1 green capsicum, thinly sliced

1/2 cup fresh sliced mushrooms

2 tablespoons dry white wine

2 tablespoons lemon juice

salt to taste

ground black pepper to taste

500g/18oz scallops

2 tablespoons grated Parmesan cheese

METHOD

1. Cook fettuccini pasta in a large pot with boiling salted water until al dente. Drain. Stir in pesto sauce and 2 tablespoons of olive oil.

2. Meanwhile, in a large skillet, sauté onion and garlic in olive oil until soft. Add green capsicum, mushrooms and cook for 3 minutes, or until soft. Stir in dry white wine, lemon juice, salt and pepper to taste, and bring to a boil. Add scallops and toss for 2 minutes. Take care not to overcook the scallops, as they will toughen when exposed to prolonged heat.

3. Toss the pesto covered pasta with the scallop sauce. Sprinkle with grated Parmesan cheese. Serve immediately.

Serves 4—6

Oyster Casserole

INGREDIENTS

6 tablespoons oil

1/2 small onion, sliced

115g/4oz fresh mushrooms, sliced

4 tablespoons plain flour

1 teaspoon salt

1 teaspoon paprika

dash of cayenne

2 cups milk

2 dozen raw oysters, with their juice

3 hard-boiled eggs, sliced

2 tablespoons cooking sherry

METHOD

1. Heat oil, add onions and mushrooms. Cook until tender and remove from pan. Blend flour with oil lining the pan. Add seasonings, fry for 2 minutes then add milk gradually.

2. Cook oysters in their own liquor until edges curl. Add oysters and liquor to mixture. Add mushrooms, onion and eggs then stir in sherry. Turn into greased casserole and bake at 200°C/400°F for 15 minutes. Serve on toast or pastry shells.

Serves 4

Sauté of Scallops

INGREDIENTS

30g/1oz butter

1 large onion, chopped

2 teaspoons freshly crushed garlic

680g/24oz scallops

3 tablespoons plain flour

1 teaspoon Madras curry powder

pepper and salt

1cup milk

chopped parsley, for garnish

METHOD

1. In a large pan, melt the butter. Sauté onion and garlic until onion is soft.

2. Beard scallops, and rinse well. Dry, and toss in flour mixed with curry powder, pepper and salt.

3. Sauté scallops in pan with garlic and onion until scallops are golden. Stir in milk.

4. Bring mixture to boil, then simmer for a few minutes or until scallops are just tender.

5. Sprinkle with chopped parsley to serve.

Serves 5–6

OYSTER CASSEROLE

Oysters Marinated with Bacon

INGREDIENTS

2 tablespoons soy sauce

$1/2$ teaspoon Worcestershire sauce

1 tablespoon honey

4 rashers rindless back bacon,
   cut into 3cm/$1^1/_4$ in -long strips

2 dozen oysters, shells discarded

12 small wooden skewers

METHOD

1. In a small bowl combine soy sauce,
Worcestershire sauce, and honey, set aside.

2. Wrap a bacon strip around each oyster,
then thread 2 wrapped oysters onto each
skewer. Place skewers in a foil-lined grill pan.
Pour marinade over oysters, cover and leave
for 30 minutes.

3. Cook oysters under a preheated grill until
bacon is golden. Serve immediately.

Makes 12

Grilled Scallops with Salsa

INGREDIENTS

30 scallops

chilli or lime oil

crisp tortilla chips

Pineapple Salsa

115g/4oz chopped pineapple

1/4 red capsicum, finely chopped

2 medium green chillies, chopped

1 tablespoon fresh coriander leaves

1 tablespoon fresh mint leaves

1 tablespoon lime juice

METHOD

1. To make salsa, place pineapple, red capsicum, chillies, coriander, mint and lime juice in a bowl. Toss to combine, then stand for 20 minutes.

2. Brush scallops with oil and cook on a preheated hot char-grill or barbecue plate (griddle) for 30 seconds on each side or until scallops just change colour. Serve immediately with salsa and tortilla chips.

Serves 4

Scallop Casserole

INGREDIENTS

500g/18oz scallops

1/4 cup chopped onions

1 can cream of mushroom soup

1/2 cup milk

1/2 –1 tsp curry powder

1/4 teaspoon pepper

1 cup shredded cheese

1 bunch asparagus, cut into 4cm/2in lengths

2 tablespoons melted butter

1 cup bread cubes

parsley

lemon rind, grated

METHOD

1. Thaw scallops if frozen. Wash scallops and drain well. Simmer scallops in boiling water. Drain. Sauté onions. Add soup, milk, curry, pepper and half of the cheese. Stir until cheese melts.

2. Slice scallops and add to soup mix along with asparagus. Add bread cubes that have been dipped in melted butter. Sprinkle with remaining cheese. Bake in 215°C/425°F oven for 15 minutes or until golden.

2. Remove from oven and sprinkle with chopped parsley and lemon rind prior to serving

Serves 4

Creamed Scallops

INGREDIENTS

680g/24oz scallops

1cup dry white wine

1/2 cup water

1 teaspoon lemon juice

15g/1/2oz butter

1 tablespoon plain flour

1 cup milk

1/2 cup cream

salt and pepper

pinch cayenne pepper

6 deep scallop shells

1 cup cheese, grated

METHOD

1. Poach scallops in wine, water and lemon juice for 3–4 minutes. Cool, strain off liquid, and reserve.

2. Melt butter, add flour and cook, stirring, for 2 minutes. Gradually stir in the reserved liquid and milk. Stir until boiling.

3. Cook rapidly for 4–5 minutes. Add cream and boil again,until thick. Season with salt, pepper and cayenne pepper.

4. Add scallops and spoon into 6 deep scallop shells. Sprinkle with cheese.

5. Brown under grill.

Serves 4–6

Garlic Scallops

INGREDIENTS

1 medium sized onion, diced finely

4—6 cloves garlic, finely chopped

1 tablespoon olive oil

500g/18oz scallop flesh

100mL/3¹/2fl oz pouring cream

4 spring onions, sliced Chinese style (on an angle)

55mL/2fl oz white wine

1 tablespoon finely chopped chives or parsley

METHOD

1. Fry garlic and onion with oil in a medium hot pan for 2 minutes, but don't allow to colour. Add scallops and lightly cook on one side for 20 seconds. Turn scallops over and cook for another 20 seconds and then remove from pan.

2. On medium to high heat, add the splash of white wine to pan and reduce for 1 minute. Add cream and reduce until the sauce thickens.

3. Add scallops, spring onions and gently toss in sauce for about 1 minute. Place scallops on big mound of rice pilaf, pour the sauce over, then garnish with chives or parsley.

Serves 4—6

Note: This lovely dish can be enlarged by the addition of prawns and/or fillets of fish.

Scallops with Plum Glaze

INGREDIENTS

680g/24oz scallops

8 bamboo skewers

3 tablespoons plum sauce

1¹/2 tablespoons lemon juice

¹/2 teaspoon lemon rind, grated

sprinkling lemon pepper seasoning

METHOD

1. Wash and clean scallops. Thread evenly onto 8 skewers.

2. Combine plum sauce, lemon juice, lemon rind and lemon pepper. Stir well to combine.

3. Place scallops under grill and baste with sauce mixture. Turn once.

4. Cook for a minute or less on each side.

Serves 4–6

Scallop Quiche

INGREDIENTS

680g/1¹/₂lb scallops (cut large scallops in half)

2 tablespoons vermouth

2 tablespoons minced parsley or chives

¹/₄ teaspoons dried thyme

23cm/9in pastry pie crust

5 eggs, beaten

1 cup light cream

¹/₄ to ¹/₂ a medium red capsicum, thinly julienned

paprika

salt and pepepr

METHOD

1. Preheat oven to 230°C/450°F. In a bowl, mix scallops, vermouth, parsley or chives, thyme, salt and pepper. Fill quiche pastry with scallop mixture. In a separate bowl, mix cream and eggs then pour over scallop mixture.

2. Arrange red capsicum slices on top and sprinkle with paprika. Bake for 10 minutes. Lower heat to 180°C/350°F and continue baking for 25-30 minutes until done. To check if quiche is cooked, insert a knife into centre. If knife comes out clean, quiche is done.

Serves 6

Spaghettini and Scallops with Breadcrumbs

INGREDIENTS

12 fresh scallops with their corals

115mL/4fl oz extra virgin olive oil

55g/2oz dried white breadcrumbs

4 tablespoons chopped fresh flat-leaf parsley

2 cloves garlic, finely chopped

1 teaspoon crushed dried chillies

340g/12oz dried spaghettini

salt

4 tablespoons dry white wine

METHOD

1. Detach the corals from the scallops and set aside. Slice the white part of each scallop into 3 or 4 pieces. Heat 2 tablespoons of oil in a frying pan, then add the breadcrumbs and fry, stirring, for 3 minutes or until golden. Remove from the pan and set aside.

2. Heat 5 tablespoons of oil in the pan, then add half the parsley and garlic and chilli and fry for 2 minutes or until the flavours are released. Meanwhile, cook pasta in plenty of boiling salted water, until al dente. Drain, return to the saucepan and toss with remaining oil.

3. Stir-fry the white parts of the scallops for 30 seconds or until they are starting to turn opaque. Add wine and reserved scallop corals and cook for 30 seconds. Add the spaghettini and cook for 1 minute, tossing to combine. Sprinkle with breadcrumbs and remaining parsley.

Serves 4

Scallop Seviche

INGREDIENTS

1½ teaspoons ground cumin

1 cup fresh lime juice

½ cup fresh orange juice

900g/2 lb bay scallops

1 hot red chilli pepper

¼ cup red onion, finely chopped

3 ripe plum tomatoes

1 red capsicum, seeded and chopped

3 spring onions, chopped

1 cup coriander, chopped

1 lime, sliced for garnish

METHOD

1. Stir the cumin into the lime and orange juice and pour over the scallops.

2. Stir in the chopped chilli pepper and red onion. Cover and refrigerate for at least 2 hours.

3. Just before serving, drain the scallops and mix with the chopped tomatoes, capsicum, spring onions and coriander. Garnish with the slices of lime.

Serves 4

Note: Hot red chilli pepper should be finely chopped. Plum tomatoes should be seeded and chopped.

Simple Scallops

INGREDIENTS

2 tablespoons, olive oil

1 clove, garlic

500g/18oz scallops, with their liquid

1 teaspoon, dried thyme

⅛ teaspoon, red pepper flakes

¼ cup white wine

METHOD

1. Heat olive oil in large pan or skillet. (Pan should be large enough to hold scallops on one layer.) Peel the garlic clove and cut into four pieces. Drain scallops and reserve the liquid.

2. Add thyme, pepper flakes, and garlic to the hot oil. Simmer gently for 3–4 minutes to roast the spices. Remove the garlic pieces if they turn brown.

3. Add white wine and scallop juice to pan. Cover and simmer 10 minutes to develop flavours.

4. Add scallops to the pan. Cover and simmer until done, about 5 minutes. Turn a couple of times.

5. Scallops are cooked when they just begin to offer some resistance to the touch. If cooked too long, they toughen.

Serves 4

Note: Scallops are just fine braised with a little thyme and white wine. Our version goes a bit further, using classic Mediterranean flavours of thyme, red pepper flakes, and garlic.
These are roasted in olive oil and complement the scallop flavour nicely. Braised scallops can be held indefinitely. Refrigerate for over half an hour and reheat gently in the microwave.

SCALLOP SEVICHE

Scallops and Wilted Spinach

INGREDIENTS

170g/6oz baby English-spinach leaves

2 teaspoons sesame seeds

2 tablespoons soy sauce

1 tablespoon lemon juice

2 teaspoons sesame oil

18 scallops

vegetable oil

crushed black peppercorns

METHOD

1. Preheat barbecue to a medium heat.

2. To make salad, blanch spinach leaves in boiling water for 10 seconds. Drain spinach, refresh under cold running water, drain again and place in a bowl.

3. Place sesame seeds, soy sauce, lemon juice and sesame oil in a bowl and mix to combine. Spoon dressing over spinach and toss to combine. Divide salad between serving plates.

4. Place scallops in bowl, drizzle with a little vegetable oil and season to taste with black pepper. Sear scallops on barbecue plate (griddle) for 45–60 seconds or until golden and flesh is opaque. Place scallops on top of each portion of salad and serve immediately.

Serves 6

Note: Alternatively the scallops can be seared in a hot frying pan.

Cajun Seafood Pasta

INGREDIENTS

500g/18oz dry fettucine pasta

2 cups double whipping cream

1 tablespoon fresh basil, chopped

1 tablespoon fresh thyme, chopped

2 teaspoons salt

2 teaspoons ground black pepper

1^1/$_2$ teaspoons crushed capsicum flakes

1 teaspoon ground white pepper

1 cup green onions, chopped

1 cup parsley, chopped

225g/8oz prawns, peeled and deveined

225g/8oz scallops

^{1}/$_2$ cup Swiss cheese, shredded

^{1}/$_2$ cup grated Parmesan cheese

METHOD

1. Cook pasta in a large pot of boiling salted water until al dente.

2. Meanwhile, pour cream into large skillet. Cook over medium heat, stirring constantly, until nearly boiling. Reduce heat, and add herbs, salt, peppers, onions, and parsley. Simmer 7–8 minutes, or until thickened.

3. Stir in seafood, cooking until prawns are no longer transparent. Stir in cheeses, blending well.

4. Drain pasta. Pour sauce over pasta.

Serves 4–6

CAJUN SEAFOOD PASTA

Scallop Thermidor

INGREDIENTS

100g/3^1/$_2$oz canned button mushrooms,
quartered

^{1}/$_4$ cup butter or margarine, melted

^{1}/$_4$ cup plain flour

1 teaspoon salt

^{1}/$_2$ teaspoon dry mustard

2 cups milk

500g/18oz cooked scallops

2 tablespoon parsley or chives, chopped

1 dash Cayenne pepper

Parmesan cheese (grated)

paprika

METHOD

1. Sauté mushrooms in butter for 5 minutes
then stir in flour and seasonings.

2. Add milk gradually and cook until thick,
stirring constantly.

3. Add scallops, parsley and cayenne pepper.

4. Place in 6 well buttered shells or 150mL/5oz
custard cups.

5. Sprinkle with cheese and paprika.

6. Bake at 200°C/400°F. for 10–15 minutes,
until cheese is browned.

Serves 6

Scallop Stir-Fry

INGREDIENTS

1 tablespoon olive oil

3–4 drops sesame oil

medium sized onion, finely sliced

2 cloves garlic, crushed

1 teaspoon fresh ginger, finely chopped

1 small red capsicum, sliced

1 small green capsicum, sliced

200g/7oz broccoli florets

55g/2oz bean sprout shoots

4 spring onions, sliced

1 tablespoon oyster sauce

1 tablespoon light soy sauce

1 fresh chilli or a teaspoon of chilli sauce

1¹/₂ cups of water, thickened with 2 teaspoons of cornflour

500g/18oz scallop flesh Chinese style (on an angle)

20 coriander leaves (optional)

METHOD

1. Heat oils in wok or frying pan, add onions, garlic and ginger and stir-fry over medium heat for 30 seconds. Add capsicum, broccoli, sprouts and spring onions and stir-frying a further 2 minutes on high heat.

2. Add scallops and sauces and stir fry for 1 minute. Add cornflour water and stir until mixture thickens.

3. Toss in coriander leaves and serve with boiled rice.

Serves 4

Scallops Fenton

INGREDIENTS

1½ cups dry white wine

2 tablespoons fresh lemon juice

1⅓ kg/3lb scallops

340g/12oz mushrooms, sliced

1 small green capsicum, sliced

¼ cup butter

½ teaspoon salt

dash freshly ground pepper

4 tablespoons plain flour

1 cup diced Swiss cheese

½ cup grated Romano cheese

1 cup cream, whipped

2 tablespoons butter for topping

paprika

METHOD

1. Bring wine and lemon juice to boil and add scallops, mushrooms, and green capicum. Simmer until scallops are just tender. Be careful not to overcook. Drain, reserving liquid. Melt butter in saucepan then blend in salt, pepper, and flour until bubbly. Gradually stir in reserved liquid and cook until thickened.

2. Add Swiss cheese and half of the Romano and stir over very low heat until blended. Remove from heat and fold in whipped cream.

3. Stir in scallop mixture, then divide amongst eight, individual, buttered scallop shells/baking dishes. Sprinkle tops with remaining Romano, dot with butter and sprinkle with paprika. Place under griller and cook until golden brown.

Serves 4

Scallops with Pea Pods and Corn

INGREDIENTS

340g/12oz fresh or frozen sea scallops

⅔ cup water

2 tablespoons dry sherry

1 tablespoon cornflour

2 teaspoons soy sauce

1 teaspoon grated fresh ginger

½ teaspoon instant chicken stock granules

1 tablespoon cooking oil

2 cups fresh pea pods, strings removed, or one 170g/6oz package frozen pea pods, thawed

115g/4oz frozen whole baby sweet corn, thawed, or one 250g/8¾oz can whole baby sweet corn, drained

16 cherry tomatoes, cut into quarters

3 green onions, sliced (⅓ cup)

2 cups hot cooked ramen or other fine noodles

METHOD

1. Thaw scallops, if frozen. Cut any large scallops in half and set aside.

2. For sauce, stir together water, sherry, cornflour, soy sauce, ginger, and stock granules in a small bowl. Set aside.

3. Pour cooking oil into a wok or large skillet. (Add more oil as necessary during cooking.) Preheat over medium-high heat. Stir-fry fresh pea pods (if using) and corn in hot oil for 1–2 minutes or until crisp-tender. Remove vegetables from the wok.

4. Add scallops to the hot wok. Stir-fry for 2 minutes or until scallops turn opaque. Push scallops from the center of the wok.

5. Stir sauce and pour into the centre of the wok. Cook and stir until thickened and bubbly. Return cooked vegetables to the wok. Add thawed frozen pea pods (if using) tomatoes, and green onions. Stir all ingredients together to coat with sauce. Cook and stir 1–2 minutes more or until heated through. Serve immediately over hot cooked noodles.

Serves 4.

SCALLOPS FENTON

SCALLOPS TARRAGON

Scallops Tarragon

INGREDIENTS

500g/18oz mixed or jumbo scallops

2 tablespoons butter or margarine

1/4 cup sliced green onion

100g/3¹/₂oz sugar snap peas

1/4 teaspoon dried tarragon, crushed

1 tablespoon dry white wine

hot cooked rice

METHOD

1. Thaw the scallops. Make sure to cut jumbo scallops in half.

2. Rinse and pat dry with paper towels.

3. In a skillet, heat butter or margarine over medium-high heat. Add the green onion and stir-fry for 1 minute. Then push the onion to one side.

4. Add scallops, sugar snap peas and tarragon. Cook stirring frequently for 5–6 minutes or until scallops are opaque and most of the liquid has evaporated.

5. Stir in white wine and sprinkle with freshly ground black pepper.
Serve with hot cooked rice.

Serves 2

Braised Scallops with Peas, Ham and Onion Sauce

INGREDIENTS

1/2 cup, frozen peas

sprinkle, sugar

1 clove, garlic

500g/18oz scallops with their liquid

3 tablespoons, olive oil

1/2 teaspoon, dried thyme

red chilli flakes sprinkle for hotness desired

3/4 cup onions, chopped coarsely

2 tablespoons ham, cooked and diced

1/3 cup white wine and scallop juice

1/3 cup water, more if needed

arrowroot or cornflour, 1 teaspoon per cup of liquids

METHOD

1. Set frozen peas in a bowl to thaw at room temperature. Sprinkle in a teaspoon of sugar. (To thaw quickly, place in a pan with a tablespoon of water. Heat covered a couple of minutes.)

2. Peel the garlic clove and cut into four pieces. Drain the scallops and reserve liquid.

3. Warm olive oil in sauté pan, or skillet, with cover large enough to hold scallops in one layer. Add thyme, chilli flakes, and garlic. Simmer gently three or four minutes to roast the spices. Remove the garlic pieces if they become brown at any point.

4. Add chopped onions and ham. Cook until the onions soften (about 5 minutes).

5. Add white wine, scallop juice, and water to pan. Cover and simmer 10 minutes to develop flavours. Add tablespoons of water if running dry.

6. Add scallops to the pan. Cover and simmer for, about 5 minutes. Turn a couple of times.

7. Scallops are done when they just begin to offer some resistance to the touch. If cooked too long, they toughen.

8. If thickening is desired add cornflour and water.
Serves 4

Scallops with Zucchini in Apple Butter

INGREDIENTS

2 zucchini, cut into 2¹/2cm/1in thick slices

8 large scallops with their corals

1 tablespoon olive oil

salt and black pepper

100mL/3¹/2fl oz apple juice

30g/1oz butter

fresh flat-leaf parsley to garnish

METHOD

1. Coat the zucchini slices and scallops gently in the oil and season.

2. Heat a large heavy-based frying pan until hot, add the zucchini slices and cook for 2 minutes on one side. Turn the zucchini over and add the scallops to the pan. Cook for 1 minute, then turn the scallops over. Cook for a further minute, until the scallops are golden and the zucchinis are browned.

3. Remove the scallops and zucchini slices from the pan and keep warm. Pour the apple juice into the pan, add the butter and cook until reduced to a syrupy sauce. Spoon the sauce over the scallops and zucchini slices and garnish with parsley.

Serves 4

Baked Scallops

INGREDIENTS

1 can cream of mushroom soup

$2/3$ cup milk

115g/8oz cracker biscuits

$3/4$ teaspoon each of garlic powder,
   oregano and thyme

500g/18oz bay scallops

paprika

METHOD

1. Preheat oven to 190°C/375°F. In a
23cm/9in round dish, mix soup with milk
and set aside. Break up third of the
crackers and mix a one third of the spices.
Coat each of scallops in the spice mixture
then place scallops in dish with soup
mixture. Break up the remainder of the
crackers into very fine pieces and mix well
with the remaining spices. Sprinkle mixture
evenly over the top of the scallops. Sprinkle
paprika over the top and bake for 30–35
minutes.

2. You may put the dish under the griller
for a couple of minutes to create a light
crust on top. Serve with rice. Good with a
green vegetable and salad.

Serves 4

Scallops with White Butter Sauce

INGREDIENTS

680g/1¹/₂lb scallops

salt and freshly ground pepper

1¹/₂ cups white wine

a little lemon juice

85g/3oz snow peas or thinly sliced green beans

1 tablespoon green onion, chopped

115g/4oz butter, cut in pieces

a few chives to garnish

METHOD

1. Remove any beards from the scallops then wash. Carefully remove the roes and lay on paper towels to dry. Season with salt and pepper. Poach the scallops and roes in wine and lemon juice for approximately 2 minutes. Remove and keep warm.

2. String snow peas or green beans and drop into boiling salted water for 1 minute then drain. Add the green onion to the poaching liquid and reduce to about ¹/₂ cup Over a gentle heat, add butter, a little at a time, whisking it in to make a sauce the consistency of pouring cream.

3. Serve with crusty bread to mop up the lovely sauce.

Serves 4

Scallop or Prawns Curry

INGREDIENTS

1 cup onion, chopped

1 whole apple, peeled and chopped

2 cloves garlic, minced

1 tablespoon curry powder

2 tablespoons margarine

¹/₄ cup flour

¹/₂ teaspoon salt

¹/₄ teaspoon cardamom

¹/₄ teaspoon pepper, freshly ground

1¹/₅ cups nonfat chicken broth

1 tablespoon lime juice, fresh

570g/1¹/₄ lb scallops/or prawns

1 cup mushroom, sliced

METHOD

1. In a large skillet, sauté onion, apple, garlic, and curry powder in margarine until tender.

2. Remove skillet from heat and blend in flour, salt, cardamom, and pepper. Stir in chicken broth and lime juice until curry sauce is well blended. Bring curry sauce to a boil, reduce heat, and simmer, uncovered for about 5 minutes, stirring occasionally.

3. Meanwhile, place scallops or shrimp in a pot of boiling water and cook for 5–10 minutes until just tender. Drain and set aside.

4. When curry sauce is finished cooking, add shellfish and mushrooms and serve over rice.

Serves 4

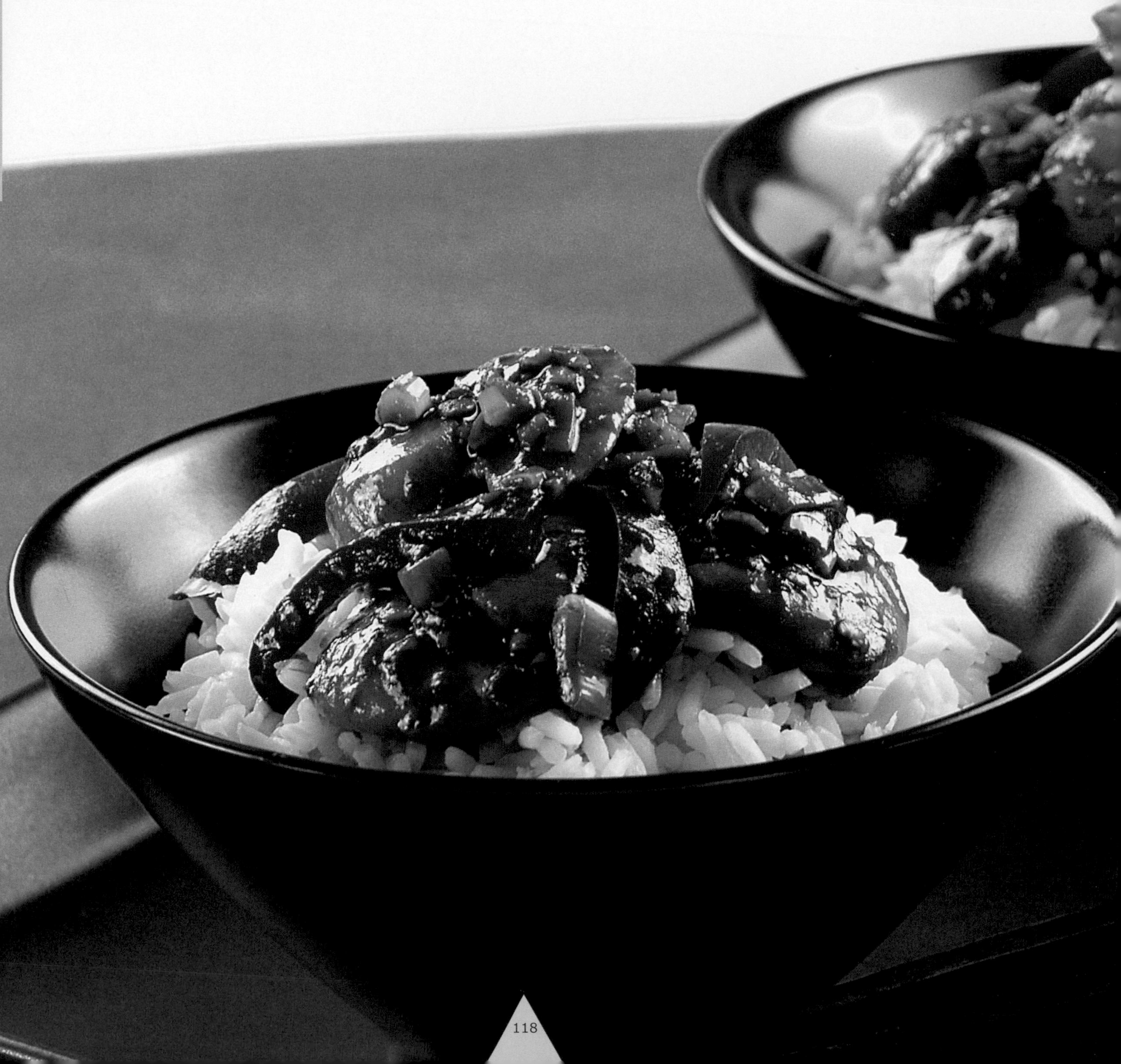

Sichuan Style Scallops

INGREDIENTS

1½ tablespoons groundnut oil

1 tablespoon ginger, finely chopped

1 tablespoon garlic, finely chopped

2 tablespoons spring onions, finely chopped

500g/18oz scallops, including corals

Sauce

1 tablespoon rice wine or dry sherry

2 teaspoons light soy sauce

2 teaspoons dark soy sauce

2 tablespoons chilli bean sauce

2 teaspoons tomato puree

1 teaspoon sugar

½ teaspoon salt

½ teaspoon sugar

2 teaspoons sesame oil

METHOD

1. Heat wok until very hot. Add the oil and when it is very hot add the ginger, garlic and spring onions. Stir-fry for 10 seconds. Add the scallops and stir-fry for 1 minute.

2. Add all the sauce ingredients except the sesame oil. Stir fry for 4 minutes until the scallops are firm and thoroughly coated with the sauce.

3. Add the sesame oil and stir-fry for another minute. Serve at once with plain rice.

Serves 4

Steak and Oyster Pot Pie

INGREDIENTS

680g/24oz lean round or topside steak, trimmed and diced of visible fat

55g/2oz plain flour, seasoned with black pepper

1 tablespoon olive oil

1 onion, diced

1 large carrot, chopped

1 parsnip, chopped

2 stalks celery, chopped

1/4 cup no-added-salt tomato paste

1 cup red wine

1 cup beef stock

1/2 cup strong coffee

1 teaspoon no-added-salt Worcestershire sauce

12 fresh oysters or 2 x 85g/3oz canned smoked oysters, rinsed and drained

3 tablespoons fresh parsley, chopped

2 tablespoons cornflour blended with 1/4 cup water

1/2 quantity ricotta pastry (see below)

Ricotta Pastry

2 cups self-raising flour

1/2 cup low-fat ricotta cheese

1/2 cup buttermilk

1 egg white

2 tablespoons unsaturated oil

1–2 tablespoons chilled skim milk

METHOD

1. Place meat and flour in a plastic food bag. Toss to coat.

2. Heat half the oil in a large non-stick frying pan over a medium heat. Add onion, carrot, parsnip and celery. Cook, stirring, for 3 minutes or until vegetables are soft. Remove vegetables from pan. Set aside.

3. Add remaining oil to pan and heat. Shake excess flour from meat. Add meat to pan. Cook, turning several times, until brown on all sides. Stir in tomato paste and cook for 3–4 minutes or until it becomes deep red and develops a rich aroma. Return vegetables to pan. Add wine, stock, coffee and Worcestershire sauce. Cover and cook over a low heat, stirring occasionally, for 20 minutes.

4. Stir in oysters, parsley and cornflour mixture. Cook, stirring, for 2–3 minutes or until mixture thickens. Remove pan from heat and allow to cool.

5. Preheat oven to 190°C/370°F. Transfer meat mixture to a deep pie dish. Roll out pastry and place over meat mixture. Bake for 20 minutes or until pastry is golden. Alternatively, bake in individual pie dishes. Serve with a green salad and crusty bread.

Ricotta Pastry

1. Place flour, ricotta cheese, buttermilk, egg white and oil in food processor. Using the pulse button, process until just combined.

2. With machine running, slowly add skim milk until mixture forms a dough.

3. Turn pastry onto a lightly floured surface. Knead into a ball. Wrap pastry in plastic food wrap. Refrigerate for at least 30 minutes or until ready to use.

Makes enough to cover a 20cm/8in round pie

Serves 6

WEIGHTS & MEASURES

Cooking is not an exact science: one does not require finely calibrated scales, pipettes and scientific equipment to cook, yet the conversion to metric measures in some countries and its interpretations must have intimidated many a good cook.

Weights are given in the recipes only for ingredients such as meats, fish, poultry and some vegetables. Though a few grams/ounces one way or another will not affect the success of your dish.

Though recipes have been tested using the Australian Standard 250mL cup, 20mL tablespoon and 5mL teaspoon, they will work just as well with the US and Canadian 8fl oz cup, or the UK 300mL cup. We have used graduated cup measures in preference to tablespoon measures so that proportions are always the same. Where tablespoon measures have been given, these are not crucial measures, so using the smaller tablespoon of the US or UK will not affect the recipe's success. At least we all agree on the teaspoon size.

For breads, cakes and pastries, the only area which might cause concern is where eggs are used, as proportions will then vary. If working with a 250mL or 300mL cup, use large eggs (60g/2oz), adding a little more liquid to the recipe for 300mL cup measures if it seems necessary. Use the medium-sized eggs (55g/1^1/2oz) with 8fl oz cup measure. A graduated set of measuring cups and spoons is recommended, the cups in particular for measuring dry ingredients. Remember to level such ingredients to ensure their accuracy.

English Measures

All measurements are similar to Australian with two exceptions: the English cup measures 300mL/10fl oz, whereas the Australian cup measure 250mL/8fl oz. The English tablespoon (the Australian dessertspoon) measures 14.8mL/**1/2**fl oz against the Australian tablespoon of 20mL/3/4fl oz.

American Measures

The American reputed pint is 16fl oz, a quart is equal to 32fl oz and the American gallon, 128fl oz. The Imperial measurement is 20fl oz to the pint, 40fl oz a quart and 160fl oz one gallon. The American tablespoon is equal to 14.8mL/^{1}/2 fl oz, the teaspoon is 5mL/^{1}/6 fl oz. The cup measure is 250mL/8fl oz, the same as Australia.

Dry Measures

All the measures are level, so when you have filled a cup or spoon, level it off with the edge of a knife. The scale below is the 'cook's equivalent'; it is not an exact conversion of metric to imperial measurement. To calculate the exact metric equivalent yourself, use 2.2046lb = 1kg or 1lb = 0.45359kg

Metric	Imperial
g = grams	oz = ounces
kg = kilograms	lb = pound
15g	^{1}/2oz
20g	^{2}/3oz
30g	1oz
55g	2oz
85g	3oz
115g	4oz/^{1}/4 lb
145g	5oz
170g	6oz
200g	7oz
225g	8oz/^{1}/2 lb
255g	9oz
285g	10oz
310g	11oz
340g	12oz/^{3}/4 lb
370g	13oz
400g	14oz
425g	15oz
1,000g	1kg/ 35.2oz/2.2 lb
1.5kg	3.3 lb

WEIGHTS & MEASURES

Oven Temperatures

The Celsius temperatures given here are not exact; they have been rounded off and are given as a guide only. Follow the manufacturer's temperature guide, relating it to oven description given in the recipe. Remember gas ovens are hottest at the top, electric ovens at the bottom and convection-fan forced ovens are usually even throughout. We included Regulo numbers for gas cookers which may assist.

To convert °C to °F multiply °C by 9 and divide by 5 then add 32.

Oven temperatures

	C°	F°	Regular
Very slow	120	250	1
Slow	150	300	2
Moderately slow	160	325	3
Moderate	180	350	4
Moderately hot	190–200	370–400	5–6
Hot	210–220	410–440	6–7
Very hot	230	450	8
Super hot	250–290	475–500	9–10

Cake dish sizes

Metric	Imperial
15cm	6in
18cm	7in
20cm	8in
23cm	9in

Loaf dish sizes

Metric	Imperial
23x12cm	9x5in
25x8cm	10x3in
28x18cm	11x7in

Liquid Measurements

The scale following is the 'cook's equivalent'; it is not an exact conversion of metric to imperial measurement. To calculate the exact equivalent yourself, divide millilitres by 28.349523 to obtain fluid ounce equivelant, or multiply fluid ounces by 28.349523 to obtain millilitre equivalant.

Liquid measures

Metric millilitres mL	Imperial fl oz	Cup & Spoon fluid ounce
5mL	$1/6$ fl oz	1 teaspoon
20mL	$2/3$ fl oz	1 tablespoon
30mL	1fl oz	(1 tablespoon plus 2 teaspoons)
60mL	2fl oz	$1/4$ cup
100mL	3fl oz	$1/3$ cup
125mL	4fl oz	$1/2$ cup
150mL	5fl oz	
250mL	8fl oz	1 cup
300mL	10fl oz	
380mL	12fl oz	$1^1/2$ cups
400mL	14fl oz	$1^3/4$ cups
500mL	16fl oz	2 cups
600mL	20fl oz	$2^1/2$ cups
1 litre	36fl oz	4 cups

Cup measurements

One cup is equal to the following weights.

	Metric	Imperial
Almonds, flaked	90g	3oz
Almonds, slivered, ground	115g	4oz
Almonds, kernel	145g	5oz
Apples, dried, chopped	115g	4oz
Apricots, dried, chopped	170g	6oz
Breadcrumbs, packet	115g	4oz
Breadcrumbs, soft	55g	2oz
Cheese, grated	115g	4oz
Choc bits	145g	5oz
Coconut, desiccated	85g	3oz
Cornflakes	30g	1oz
Currants	145g	5oz
Flour	115g	4oz
Fruit, dried (mixed, sultanas etc)	170g	6oz
Ginger, crystallised, glace	225g	8oz

	Metric	Imperial
Honey, treacle, golden syrup	285g	10oz
Mixed peel	200g	7oz
Nuts, chopped	115g	4oz
Prunes, chopped	200g	7oz
Rice, cooked	145g	5oz
Rice, uncooked	200g	7oz
Rolled oats	85g	3oz
Sesame seeds	115g	4oz
Shortening (butter, margarine)	225g	8oz
Sugar, brown	145g	5oz
Sugar, granulated or caster	225g	8oz
Sugar, sifted icing	145g	5oz
Wheatgerm	55g	2oz

Length

Some of us still have trouble converting imperial length to metric. In this scale, measures have been rounded off to the easiest-to-use and most acceptable figures.

To obtain the exact metric equivalent in converting inches to centimetres, multiply inches by 2.54 whereby 1 inch equals 25.4 millimetres and 1 millimetre equals 0.03937 inches.

Metric mm = millimetres cm = centimetres	Imperial in = inches ft = feet
5mm, 0.5cm	$1/4$ in
10mm, 1.0cm	$1/2$ in
20mm, 2.0cm	$3/4$ in
$2^1{}_2$cm	1in
5cm	2in
$7^1{}_2$cm	3in
10cm	4in
$12^1{}_2$cm	5in
15cm	6in
18cm	7in
20cm	8in
23cm	9in
25cm	10in
28cm	11in
30cm	1ft, 12in

GLOSSARY

acidulated water: water with added acid, such as lemon juice or vinegar, which prevents discoloration of ingredients, particularly fruit or vegetables. The proportion of acid to water is 1 teaspoon per 300mL.

al dente: Italian cooking term for ingredients that are cooked until tender but still firm to the bite; usually applied to pasta.

americaine: method of serving seafood - usually lobster and monkfish - in a sauce flavoured with olive oil, aromatic herbs, tomatoes, white wine, fish stock, brandy and tarragon.

anglaise: cooking style for simple cooked dishes such as boiled vegetables. Assiette anglaise is a plate of cold cooked meats.

antipasto: Italian for "before the meal", it denotes an assortment of cold meats, vegetables and cheeses, often marinated, served as an hors d'oeuvre. A typical antipasto might include salami, prosciutto, marinated artichoke hearts, anchovy fillets, olives, tuna fish and Provolone cheese.

au gratin: food sprinkled with breadcrumbs, often covered with cheese sauce and browned until a crisp coating forms.

balsamic vinegar: a mild, extremely fragrant wine-based vinegar made in northern Italy. Traditionally, the vinegar is aged for at least seven years in a series of casks made of various woods.

baste: to moisten food while it is cooking by spooning or brushing on liquid or fat.

baine marie: a saucepan standing in a large pan which is filled with boiling water to keep liquids at simmering point. A double boiler will do the same job.

beat: to stir thoroughly and vigorously.

beurre manie: equal quantities of butter and flour kneaded together and added a little at a time to thicken a stew or casserole.

bird: see paupiette.

blanc: a cooking liquid made by adding flour and lemon juice to water in order to keep certain vegetables from discolouring as they cook.

blanch: to plunge into boiling water and then in some cases, into cold water. Fruits and nuts are blanched to remove skin easily.

blanquette: a white stew of lamb, veal or chicken, bound with egg yolks and cream and accompanied by onion and mushrooms.

blend: to mix thoroughly.

bonne femme: dishes cooked in the traditional French "housewife" style. Chicken and pork bonne femme are garnished with bacon, potatoes and baby onion; fish bonne femme with mushrooms in a white wine sauce.

bouquet garni: a bunch of herbs, usually consisting of sprigs of parsley, thyme, marjoram, rosemary, a bay leaf, peppercorns and cloves, tied in muslin and used to flavour stews and casseroles.

braise: to cook whole or large pieces of poultry, game, fish, meat or vegetables in a small amount of wine, stock or other liquid in a closed pot. Often the main ingredient is first browned in fat and then cooked in a low oven or very slowly on top of the stove. Braising suits tough meats and older birds and produces a mellow, rich sauce.

broil: the American term for grilling food.

brown: cook in a small amount of fat until brown.

burghul (also bulgur): a type of cracked wheat, where the kernels are steamed and dried before being crushed.

buttered: to spread with softened or melted butter.

butterfly: to slit a piece of food in half horizontally, cutting it almost through so that when opened it resembles butterfly wings. Chops, large prawns and thick fish fillets are often butterflied so that they cook more quickly.

buttermilk: a tangy, low-fat cultured milk product whose slight acidity makes it an ideal marinade base for poultry.

calzone: a semicircular pocket of pizza dough, stuffed with meat or vegetables, sealed and baked.

caramelise: to melt sugar until it is a golden brown syrup.

champignons: small mushrooms, usually canned.

chasseur: (hunter) a French cooking style in which meat and chicken dishes are cooked with mushrooms, shallots, white wine, and often tomato.

clarify: to melt butter and drain the oil off the sediment.

coat: to cover with a thin layer of flour, sugar, nuts, crumbs, poppy or sesame seeds, cinnamon sugar or a few of the ground spices.

concasser: to chop coarsely, usually tomatoes.

confit: from the French verb confire, meaning to preserve. Food that is made into a preserve by cooking very slowly and thoroughly until tender. In the case of meat, such as duck or goose, it is cooked in its own fat, and covered with it so that it does not come into contact with the air. Vegetables such as onions are good inconfit.

consomme: a clear soup usually made from beef.

coulis: a thin puree, usually of fresh or cooked fruit or vegetables, which is soft enough to pour (couler means to run). A coulis may be rough-textured or very smooth.

court bouillon: the liquid in which fish, poultry or meat is cooked. It usually consists of water with bay leaf, onion, carrots and salt and freshly ground black pepper to taste. Other additives can include wine, vinegar, stock, garlic or spring onions (scallions).

couscous: cereal processed from semolina into pellets, traditionally steamed and served with meat and vegetables in the classic North African stew of the same name.

cruciferous vegetables: certain members of the mustard, cabbage and turnip families with cross-shaped flowers and strong aromas and flavours.

cream: to make soft, smooth and creamy by rubbing with back of spoon or by beating with mixer. Usually applied to fat and sugar.

croutons: small toasted or fried cubes of bread.

crudites: raw vegetables, whether cut in slices or sticks to nibble plain or with a dipping sauce, or shredded and tossed as salad with a simple dressing.

cube: to cut into small pieces with 6 equal sides.

curdle: to cause milk or sauce to separate into solid and liquid. Example, overcooked egg mixtures.

daikon radish (also called mooli): a long white Japanese radish.

dark sesame oil (also called Oriental sesame oil): dark polyunsaturated oil with a low burning point, used for seasoning. Do not replace with lighter sesame oil.

deglaze: to dissolve congealed cooking juices or glaze on the bottom of a pan by adding a liquid, then scraping and stirring vigorously whilst bringing the liquid to the boil. Juices may be used to make gravy or to add to sauce.

degrease: to skim grease from the surface of liquid. If possible the liquid should be chilled so the fat solidifies. If not, skim off most of the fat with a large metal spoon, then trail strips of paper towel on the surface of the liquid to remove any remaining globules.

devilled: a dish or sauce that is highly seasoned with a hot ingredient such as mustard, Worcestershire sauce or cayenne pepper.

dice: to cut into small cubes.

dietary fibre: a plant-cell material that is undigested or only partially digested in the human body, but which promotes healthy digestion of other food matter.

dissolve: mix a dry ingredient with liquid until absorbed.

dredge: to coat with a dry ingredient, as flour or sugar.

drizzle: to pour in a fine thread-like stream over a surface.

dust: to sprinkle or coat lightly with flour or icing sugar.

Dutch oven: a heavy casserole with a lid usually made from cast iron or pottery.

emulsion: a mixture of two liquids that are not mutually soluble - for example, oil and water.

entree: in Europe, the "entry" or hors d'oeuvre; in North America entree means the main course.

fillet: special cut of beef, lamb, pork or veal; breast of poultry and game; fish cut off the bone lengthways.

flake: to break into small pieces with a fork.

flame: to ignite warmed alcohol over food.

fold in: a gentle, careful combining of a light or delicate mixture with a heavier mixture using a metal spoon.

fricassee: a dish in which poultry, fish or vegetables are bound together with a white or veloute sauce. In Britain and the United States, the name applies to an old-fashioned dish of chicken in a creamy sauce.

galette: sweet or savoury mixture shaped as a flat round.

garnish: to decorate food, usually with something edible.

gastrique: caramelized sugar deglazed with vinegar and used in fruit-flavoured savoury sauces, in such dishes as duck with orange.

glaze: a thin coating of beaten egg, syrup or aspic which is brushed over pastry, fruits or cooked meats.

gluten: a protein in flour that is developed when dough is kneaded, making it elastic.

gratin: a dish cooked in the oven or under the grill so that it develops a brown crust. Breadcrumbs or cheese may be sprinkled on top first. Shallow gratin dishes ensure a maximum area of crust.

grease: to rub or brush lightly with oil or fat.

infuse: to immerse herbs, spices or other flavourings in hot liquid to flavour it. Infusion takes from two to five minutes depending on the flavouring. The liquid should be very hot but not boiling.

jardiniere: a garnish of garden vegetables, typically carrots, pickling onions, French beans and turnips.

GLOSSARY

joint: to cut poultry, game or small animals into serving pieces by dividing at the joint.

julienne: to cut food into match-like strips.

knead: to work dough using heel of hand with a pressing motion, while stretching and folding the dough.

lights: lungs of an animal, used in various meat preparations such as pates and faggots.

line: to cover the inside of a container with paper, to protect or aid in removing mixture.

macerate: to soak food in liquid to soften.

marinade: a seasoned liquid, usually an oil and acid mixture, in which meats or other foods are soaked to soften and give more flavour.

marinara: Italian "sailor's style" cooking that does not apply to any particular combination of ingredients. Marinara tomato sauce for pasta is most familiar.

marinate: to let food stand in a marinade to season and tenderize.

mask: to cover cooked food with sauce.

melt: to heat until liquified.

mince: to grind into very small pieces.

mix: to combine ingredients by stirring.

monounsaturated fats: one of three types of fats found in foods. Are believed not to raise the level of cholesterol in the blood.

nicoise: a garnish of tomatoes, garlic and black olives; a salad with anchovy, tuna and French beans is typical.

non-reactive pan: a cooking pan whose surface does not chemically react with food. Materials used include stainless steel, enamel, glass and some alloys.

noisette: small "nut" of lamb cut from boned loin or rack that is rolled, tied and cut in neat slices. Noisette also means flavoured with hazelnuts, or butter cooked to a nut brown colour.

normande: a cooking style for fish, with a garnish of prawns (shrimp), mussels and mushrooms in a white wine cream sauce; for poultry and meat, a sauce with cream, Calvados and apple.

olive oil: various grades of oil extract from olives. Extra virgin olive oil has a full, fruity flavour and the lowest acidity. Virgin olive oil is slightly higher in acidity and lighter in flavour. Pure olive oil is a processed blend of olive oils and has the highest acidity and lightest taste.

panade: a mixture for binding stuffings and dumplings, notably quenelles, often of choux pastry or simply breadcrumbs. A panade may also be made of frangipane, pureed potatoes or rice.

papillote: to cook food in oiled or buttered greasepoof paper or aluminium foil. Also a decorative frill to cover bone ends of chops and poultry drumsticks.

parboil: to boil or simmer until part cooked (i.e. cooked further than when blanching).

pare: to cut away outside covering.

pate: a paste of meat or seafood used as a spread for toast or crackers.

paupiette: a thin slice of meat, poultry or fish spread with a savoury stuffing and rolled. In the United States this is also called "bird" and in Britain an "olive".

peel: to strip away outside covering.

plump: to soak in liquid or moisten thoroughly until full and round.

poach: to simmer gently in enough hot liquid to cover, using care to retain shape of food.

polyunsaturated fat: one of the three types of fats found in food. These exist in large quantities in such vegetable oils as safflower, sunflower, corn and soya bean. These fats lower the level of cholesterol in the blood.

puree: a smooth paste, usually of vegetables or fruits, made by putting foods through a sieve, food mill or liquefying in a blender or food processor.

ragout: traditionally a well-seasoned, rich stew containing meat, vegetables and wine. Nowadays, a term applied to any stewed mixture.

ramekins: small oval or round individual baking dishes.

reconstitute: to put moisture back into dehydrated foods by soaking in liquid.

reduce: to cook over a very high heat, uncovered, until the liquid is reduced by evaporation.

refresh: to cool hot food quickly, either under running water or by plunging it into iced water, to stop it cooking. Particularly for vegetables and occasionally for shellfish.

rice vinegar: mild, fragrant vinegar that is less sweet than cider vinegar and not as harsh as distilled malt vinegar. Japanese rice vinegar is milder than the Chinese variety.

roulade: a piece of meat, usually pork or veal, that is spread with stuffing, rolled and often braised or poached. A roulade may also be a sweet or savoury mixture that is baked in a Swiss roll tin or paper case, filled with a contrasting filling, and rolled.

rubbing-in: a method of incorporating fat into flour, by use of fingertips only. Also incorporates air into mixture.

safflower oil: the vegetable oil that contains the highest proportion of polyunsaturated fats.

salsa: a juice derived from the main ingredient being cooked or a sauce added to a dish to enhance its flavour. In Italy the term is often used for pasta sauces; in Mexico the name usually applies to uncooked sauces served as an accompaniment, especially to corn chips.

saturated fats: one of the three types of fats found in foods. These exist in large quantities in animal products, coconut and palm oils; they raise the level of cholesterol in the blood. As high cholesterol levels may cause heart disease, saturated fat consumption is recommended to be less than 15% of kilojoules provided by the daily diet.

sauté: to cook or brown in small amount of hot fat.

score: to mark food with cuts, notches of lines to prevent curling or to make food more attractive.

scald: to bring just to boiling point, usually for milk. Also to rinse with boiling water.

sear: to brown surface quickly over high heat in hot dish.

seasoned flour: flour with salt and pepper added.

sift: to shake a dry, powdered substance through a sieve or sifter to remove any lumps and give lightness.

simmer: to cook food gently in liquid that bubbles steadily just below boiling point so that the food cooks in even heat without breaking up.

singe: to quickly flame poultry to remove all traces of feathers after plucking.

skim: to remove a surface layer (often of impurities and scum) from a liquid with a metal spoon or small ladle.

slivered: sliced in long, thin pieces, usually refers to nuts, especially almonds.

soften: re gelatine - sprinkle over cold water and allow to gel (soften) then dissolve and liquefy.

souse: to cover food, particularly fish, in wine vinegar and spices and cook slowly; the food is cooled in the same liquid. Sousing gives food a pickled flavour.

steep: to soak in warm or cold liquid in order to soften food and draw out strong flavours or impurities.

stir-fry: to cook thin slices of meat and vegetable over a high heat in a small amount of oil, stirring constantly to even cooking in a short time. Traditionally cooked in a wok, however a heavy based frying pan may be used.

stock: a liquid containing flavours, extracts and nutrients of bones, meat, fish or vegetables.

stud: to adorn with; for example, baked ham studded with whole cloves.

sugo: an Italian sauce made from the liquid or juice extracted from fruit or meat during cooking.

sweat: to cook sliced or chopped food, usually vegetables, in a little fat and no liquid over very low heat. Foil is pressed on top so that the food steams in its own juices, usually before being added to other dishes.

timbale: a creamy mixture of vegetables or meat baked in a mould. French for "kettledrum"; also denotes a drum-shaped baking dish.

thicken: to make a thin, smooth paste by mixing together arrowroot, cornflour or flour with an equal amount of cold water; stir into hot liquid, cook, stirring until thickened.

toss: to gently mix ingredients with two forks or fork spoon.

total fat: the individual daily intake of all three fats previously described in this glossary. Nutritionists recommend that fats provide no more than 35% of the energy in the diet.

vine leaves: tender, lightly flavoured leaves of the grapevine, used in ethnic cuisine as wrappers for savoury mixtures. As the leaves are usually packed in brine, they should be well rinsed before use.

whip: to beat rapidly, incorporate air and produce expansion.

zest: thin outer layer of citrus fruits containing the aromatic citrus oil. It is usually thinly pared with a vegetable peeler, or grated with a zester or grater to separate it from the bitter white pith underneath.

INDEX